FAIR

by Joy Wilkinson

'A Future Fair for All'
    The Labour Party

'A Fair Deal for Everyone'
    The Conservative Party

'Fighting for a Fairer Burnley'
    The British National Party

finboroughtheatre

First performance at the Finborough Theatre, London,
Tuesday 16th August 2005.

Floodtide presents the world premiere of

FAIR

by Joy Wilkinson

RAILTON	**Matthew Wilson**
MELANIE	**Rebecca Everett**
GEORGE	**Jonathan Jaynes**

Director	**Helen Eastman**
Designer	**James Cotterill**
Lighting Designer	**Neill Brinkworth**
Sound Designer	**Fergus Mount**
Stage Manager	**Nick Hayman-Joyce**
Assistant Director	**Dan Ayling**

The performance lasts approximately eighty minutes, without an interval.

Matthew Wilson – *Railton*
Matthew trained at LAMDA. Television credits include *Where the Heart Is, Wire in the Blood, No Angels* and *Ghost Squad*. His theatre credits include: *There* at the Royal Court as part of its *Rampage* season.

Rebecca Everett – *Melanie*
Rebecca trained at Bretton Hall (Devised Performance) and LAMDA. Previous credits include Adele in *Herons* (Landor Theatre, Clapham).

Jonathan Jaynes – *George*
Jonathan trained at LAMDA. His theatre credits include: Angus in *Neville's Island* (Wolsey Theatre, Ipswich), Judd in *Bouncers* (Hull Truck Theatre Company), Caliban in *The Tempest* (National Theatre), Gora in *Wicked Yaar!* (National Theatre), Harry Doulton in *Equus* (Salisbury Playhouse), Mike in *Wait Until Dark* (Watford Palace), Jack in *Happy Families* (Watford Palace), Levin in *Anna Karenina* (Watford Palace), Louis in *A View from the Bridge* (Wolsey Theatre, Ipswich), Diggory in *She Stoops To Conquer* (Leeds Playhouse), Tranio in *Taming Of The Shrew* (English Heritage), Macduff in *Macbeth* (Theatre Museum), Jan in *No Pasaran* (Link Studio) and Stephen in *Hard Times* (Link Studio). Television includes: most recently Mitch Hall and also Hughes in *The Bill* (Thames/Pearson), Shawn in *Down to Earth* (BBC), Edward Potts in *Oliver Twist* (Diplomat Films), Tyrhwhitt in the documentary series *Elizabeth* (Channel 4), DC Robinson in *Dream Team* (Sky), Jimmy in *EastEnders,* John Finch in *Between the Lines* (BBC), Bruno in *September Song*, Bobby in *Travelling Man* and PC Andy in *Coronation Street* (Granada). Film includes: First Guard in *First Knight* directed by Jerry Zucker and The Maniac in *Carancula* directed by Mariano Baino.

Joy Wilkinson – Writer

Joy's plays include *Felt Effects* (joint winner of the Verity Bargate Award), *Interior Design for the Undead* (winner of the International Student Playscript Competition) and *The Aquatic Ape*, performed in the 5065 Lift at the 2004 Edinburgh Festival. Her short plays have been performed at Soho Theatre, BAC, King's Head Theatre, Hen & Chickens Theatre and in Floodtide's *Change* project at the Network Theatre. This is Joy's first full production in London.

Helen Eastman – Director

Helen returns to the Finborough after her acclaimed production of *The Monument* in 2003. In the interim Helen has directed two operas: *Hansel and Gretel* at Cork Opera House and the world premiere of *Bug Off!* for a Northern Ireland tour (OTC). She has assisted Michael Attenborough at the Almeida and, for Floodtide, initiated and produced the *Change* project. She trained at LAMDA after graduating from Oxford University and directing credits include *Wild Raspberries* (The Citizens' Theatre, Glasgow), *Wolf Game* (The Union), the revival of Adrian Osmond's *Turn of the Screw* (OTC), *The Baltimore Waltz* (The Gatehouse), *The Odyssey* (site-specific) and *The Cure at Troy* (BAC and tour), a revival of which opens at the Cockpit Theatre in September 2005. She has recently been developing a production of *David's Red Haired Death* including workshops at the Young Vic Studio as part of the Genesis Programme for Young Directors. She has worked as a staff director for *English Touring Opera* and as a researcher for Michael Moore. She has been made Visiting Fellow in Theatre at Westminster University and a Projects Associate for the Almeida. She has recently become the Producer of the Onassis Programme for the Performance of Greek Drama at Oxford University.

James Cotterill – Designer

James trained in Theatre Production at RADA before completing the Motley Theatre Design Course. Recently he has designed *Big Sale* (Protein Dance), *The Fool* (Vanbrugh Theatre, RADA) and *The Cudgel and the Rapier* (Liquid Theatre/BAC). As Assistant Designer to Dick Bird he has worked on *Tejas Verdes* (The Gate), *The Gondoliers* (Deutsche Oper am Rhein, Düsseldorf), *Lear* (Sheffield Crucible), *Dirty Wonderland* (Frantic Assembly), *The Gambler* (Maastricht) and currently *Fatal Harvest* (Royal Court). Other work includes the dance pieces *Pop* (Harlow Playhouse) and *Trick or Treat* (Millfield Theatre). James has also worked as assistant art director on the Channel 4 programme *Hollyoaks* and as a buyer for the BBC.

Neill Brinkworth – Lighting Designer

Neill trained at Dartington. Lighting Designs for: The Kosh, IRIE! Dance Theatre, Context Theatre, Frontline Productions, Runaway Theatre, Candid Theatre, Second Wave, Performance 2, Connecting Vibes Dance, London Opera. Relights and Production LX includes: *The Vagina Monologues*, English Touring Opera, Out of Joint, Theatre Alibi.

Fergus Mount – Sound Designer

Fergus has just graduated from the Central School of Speech and Drama where he studied sound design and production.

Nick Hayman-Joyce – Stage Manager

Previous Stage Management includes: *Forbidden* (C venues, Edinburgh Fringe), *Three Women, Cue Deadly* (Riverside Studios), *Talkin' Loud, Stealing Sweets And Punching People* and *Miguel Street* (all Latchmere Theatre).

Dan Ayling – Assistant Director

Dan is currently studying for an MFA in Theatre Directing at Birkbeck College. Previously he worked, as DSM, at the Citizens' Theatre, Glasgow, with Philip Prowse and Giles Havergal; at Almeida Opera with Stephen Langridge and Lindsay Posner; and at Pitlochry Festival Theatre with Richard Baron and Ian Grieve, having trained at Guildhall. Recent work includes *Cricket Remixed* for Almeida Projects (a week-long intensive workshop with young people from Islington Arts and Media School) and *Mary Stuart* at Drama Centre, as assistant to Annie Tyson. Future work, as Resident Assistant Director at Hampstead Theatre, includes *Nathan the Wise* directed by Tony Clark, *Comfort Me With Apples* directed by Lucy Bailey and *The Rubenstein Kiss* directed by James Phillips.

Floodtide would like to thank the following who have made this production possible:

Floodtide's Patrons, Angels and Friends and the donors to the 2005 Annual Auction

The Peggy Ramsay Foundation

Neil Williams, Nick Aaron, Tony Guilfoyle, Sheridan Smith, Ben Evans, Dylan and Ben, Matt Peover, Anthony Shuster, Prof. Vanessa Toulmin at the National Fairground Archive, The Campaign Against Racism and Fascism, Hampstead Theatre Start Night

FLOODTIDE

www.floodtide.org.uk

Floodtide was founded in 2000 to commission and produce theatre and arts events which explored and challenged the politics and ethics of the world we live in.

Previous productions include *The Baltimore Waltz* by Paula Vogel (The Gatehouse, London), *HyperLynx* by John McGrath (The Citizens' Theatre, Glasgow, The Pleasance Edinburgh, The Tricycle, London), *Wild Raspberries* by Elizabeth MacLennan (The Citizens' Theatre, Glasgow, The Pleasance, Edinburgh), *Wolf Game* by Sarah Diamond (The Union Theatre, London), *The Cure at Troy* by Seamus Heaney (BAC and tour).

This year's main development project was *Change*. In the run-up to the 2005 UK election, thousands of people around the UK contributed their views on changing Britain and inspired ten new short plays by Jack Thorne, Nick Harrop, Matt Morrison, Samantha Ellis, Wayne Reid, Joy Wilkinson, Anthony Shuster, Vanessa Badham, Sarah Diamond and Rebecca Wojciechowski. Ten directors and forty actors came together to produce these plays at the Network Theatre.

Floodtide
Studio 41
Clink Street Studios
1 Soho Wharf
London SE1 9DG

Also in this volume

Felt Effects was joint winner of the Verity Bargate Award and was developed in a reading by Frontline at Soho Theatre. It will be premiered by Floodtide. For more information see: www.floodtide.org.uk.

finboroughtheatre

www.finboroughtheatre.co.uk

Artistic Director **Neil McPherson**
Resident Company **Concordance** www.concordance.org.uk
Associate Directors **John Terry, Kate Wasserberg**
Associate Designer **Alex Marker**
Writers-in-Residence **David Carter, James Graham, Laura Wade**
Resident Assistant Director **Kate Wasserberg**
Technical Manager **Alex Watson**
Interns **Johanna Dunphy, Robin Steinthal, Amy Vlastelica**

Founded in 1980, and celebrating its 25th anniversary in 2005, the Finborough Theatre presents new British writing, UK premieres of overseas drama, particularly from the United States, Canada and Ireland, music theatre and unjustly neglected plays from the last 150 years.

In its first decade, artists working at the theatre included Clive Barker, Kathy Burke, Ken Campbell, Mark Rylance and Clare Dowie (the world premiere of *Adult Child/Dead Child*). From 1991-1994, the theatre was at the forefront of the explosion of new writing with Naomi Wallace's first play *The War Boys*; Rachel Weisz in David Farr's *Neville Southall's Washbag* which later became the award-winning West End play, *Elton John's Glasses*; and three plays by Anthony Neilson: *The Year of the Family; Normal: the Düsseldorf Ripper*; and *Penetrator* which transferred from the Traverse and went on to play at the Royal Court Upstairs. From 1994, the theatre was run by The Steam Industry. Highlights included new plays by Tony Marchant, David Eldridge, Mark Ravenhill and Phil Willmott, new writing development including Mark Ravenhill's *Shopping and Fucking* (Royal Court, West End and Broadway) and Naomi Wallace's *Slaughter City* (Royal Shakespeare Company), the UK premiere of David Mamet's *The Woods*, and Anthony Neilson's *The Censor* which transferred to the Royal Court.

Neil McPherson became Artistic Director in 1999. *Time Out* Critics' Choice winners since then have included the UK premieres of Brad Fraser's *Wolfboy*; Lanford Wilson's *Sympathetic Magic*; Tennessee Williams' *Something Cloudy, Something Clear*; and Frank McGuinness' *Gates of Gold* with William Gaunt and the late John

Bennett in his last stage role; the London premiere of Sonja Linden's *I Have Before Me a Remarkable Document Given to Me by a Young Lady from Rwanda*; the specially commissioned adaptation of W.H. Davies' *Young Emma* by Laura Wade and directed by Tamara Harvey; Lynn Siefert's *Coyote Ugly*; the first London revival for more than 40 years of Rolf Hochhuth's *Soldiers*; and four first plays by new writers – Jason Hall's *Eyes Catch Fire*; Chris Dunkley's *Mirita*; Dameon Garnett's *Break Away* (published by Oberon Books) and Simon Vinnicombe's *Year 10* (published by Methuen). Other productions have included *Waterloo Day* with Robert Lang; Sarah Phelps' *Modern Dance for Beginners,* subsequently produced at the Soho Theatre; Carolyn Scott-Jeffs' sell-out comedy *Out in the Garden* which transferred to the Assembly Rooms, Edinburgh; the musical *Schwartz It All About*; the London premiere of Larry Kramer's *The Destiny of Me* (No 1 Critics Choice in *The Evening Standard*); *The Women's War* – an evening of original suffragette plays; Steve Hennessy's *Lullabies of Broadmoor* on the Finborough Road murder of 1922; the Victorian comedy *Masks and Faces*; *Etta Jenks* with Clarke Peters and Daniela Nardini; *The Gigli Concert* with Niall Buggy, Catherine Cusack and Paul McGann; the UK premiere of Darius Milhaud's opera *Médée*; and *Hortensia and the Museum of Dreams* with Linda Bassett.

The Finborough Theatre won the Guinness Award for Theatrical Ingenuity in 1996 and 1997; the Pearson Award bursary for writers Chris Lee in 2000 and Laura Wade in 2004; was shortlisted for the Empty Space Peter Brook Award in 2003; and won the Empty Space Peter Brook Mark Marvin Award in 2004. In 2004, the theatre was named by *Variety* as one of the top five fringe venues in London.

The Finborough Theatre is licensed by the Royal Borough of Kensington and Chelsea to The Steam Industry. The Steam Industry is under the Artistic Direction of Phil Willmott (www.philwillmott.co.uk) The Steam Industry is a company limited by guarantee. Registered in England no. 3448268. Registered Charity no. 1071304. Registered Office: 118 Finborough Road, London SW10 9ED.

FAIR

Joy Wilkinson

Characters

RAILTON, *twenty-two*

MELANIE, *twenty-one*

GEORGE, *Railton's dad, mid-forties*

The play is set in a Lancashire town.

Speeches between forward slashes (/) are spoken simultaneously by both characters.

This text went to press before the end of rehearsals so may differ slightly from the play as performed.

SCENE ONE

The fairground. A light finds RAILTON *and* MELANIE
dangling upside down, side by side, on the Revolution ride.
MELANIE *is crunched up, petrified, with her eyes shut tight.*
RAILTON *is wearing a Batman baseball cap and his arms
are spread wide as he whoops over a blasting soundtrack of
different tunes playing at once, from house to ragga, all with
banging bass.*

RAILTON. It's a rush, a blast, unreal, a dream of falling where
you don't have to wake up. I dream of fairgrounds. Or that's
just what dreams are like. Like when you're tripping and the
whole world turns into one big fairground, lights stringing
across the sky, eye-watering colours, throat-scorching
smells, everything boring bursting out Blackpool bright.
Everything's alive: the whole town, the dots down below, all
dancing like angel dust in front of my eyes. I'm alive:
dangling upside down like a baseball-capped Batman, head
fat with blood, fists punching the puddles, sucking clouds
up into my punchbag lungs, sparking up and blowing smoke
rings like UFOs over the roaring planet below. (*Strikes his
lighter and lights a roll-up.*)

MELANIE. Gripping tight to the rusted safety rail that isn't
safe, that hasn't locked. Knuckles white, eyes zipped, don't
want to see the bolts loosening or the lad beside me
sparking up in the fog of oil fumes. How can he even
breathe up here? How can he let go of the rail? How can
they put this junk up so quickly? Did that kid put it up with
his slippery little hands, little scabby Neanderthal hands
hardly off toys? Tiny assassin's hands that haven't checked
my safety rail. It's not meant to be fastened with gaffer tape.
I'm not meant to be falling forward. My brain's not meant
to be leaking through my hair. My heart's not meant to stop.
I want to get off. I don't want to die. I don't want to die . . .

The music drops to background as the ride stops at the top.

I don't want to die. I –

RAILTON. Fucking non-smokers, can't get away from them even up here.

MELANIE. Put your brain in, dickhead. This thing's covered in oil.

RAILTON. Let go of the bar, blondie. Open your eyes.

MELANIE. Shut your face. Put your fag out.

RAILTON. Take your plait out. Let it dangle.

MELANIE. Put your fag out.

RAILTON. It's not a fag. Can't you smell it?

MELANIE. I can't smell anything except oil and cheap aftershave. You're going to blow us up one way or another.

RAILTON. It's not cheap.

MELANIE. What?

RAILTON. It's nice. Smell me proper.

MELANIE. Get lost.

RAILTON. I smell nice. Go on. (*Sings along to Blu Cantrell track in the background.*) 'Breathe. Breathe. Breathe.'

Reluctantly, her eyes still shut, she turns her head and sniffs him.

It was a present. It wasn't cheap.

MELANIE. No, it's nice. / It's just strong. /

RAILTON. / It's just strong / cos your eyes are shut. Open your eyes, blondie.

He tugs her plait, she panics.

MELANIE. No!

RAILTON (*laughing, inhaling*). I think you should have a go on this. Chill you out.

MELANIE. I don't smoke fags.

RAILTON. It's not a fag. (*Blows smoke over her face.*) See?

MELANIE. Oh, yeah, that's really nice.

RAILTON. D'you want a go?

MELANIE (*pause, opens an eye and sizes him up, smiles*). Go on then.

RAILTON. You'll have to let go of the bar.

MELANIE (*freezing up, eyes shut again*). No.

RAILTON. You might as well, it don't work.

MELANIE. No!

RAILTON. Okay, open your lips at least.

She opens her mouth, he takes a moment to take her in and then puts the spliff to her lips. But when she tries to inhale, he moves it away. He teases her a couple of times until she has to open her eyes, then he grins and feeds her a drag. She grins back.

That better?

MELANIE. Yeah. Thanks. (*Fleeting relaxation passes and she freezes up again.*) When the fuck's he going to tip us back up?

RAILTON. This int Disneyland, love. No thirty quid for a thirty-second thrill which int even thrilling cos you're strapped in like a pram. This is the real deal. This baby don't stop till the bloke gets bored and it's your lucky night cos I've warned him: less than ten minutes and I'll cut his next wrap with battery acid.

MELANIE. What're you saying? Are you saying he's off his head?

RAILTON. It's better than having him nod off.

MELANIE. I want to get off.

RAILTON. Why d'you get on then?

MELANIE. I want to get off!

RAILTON. Okay, blondie. Don't cry. I wouldn't do this for just anyone you know. (*Whistles loudly and shouts down.*) Oi! Cunny mate. Bring us into land.

Blackout. Music swells again and a ride-operator ANNOUNCEMENT *calls out.*

ANNOUNCEMENT. Hold tight, boys and girls. Here we go. Here we go. Climb on board for the ride of your life. Come on, lads. Come on, lasses. Get on and cop off. Keep your arms in the car and keep your hands in each other. Hold onto your lay and hold onto your lunch. We'll be cranking it up till you're ready to chuck. Scream if you wanna go faster. Scream if you wanna go slower. It don't matter, I can't hear you for screaming and we ain't going to stop. The fun's just begun. (*Shifts tone to official.*) Warning: this ride is not suitable for bad backs, dicky tickers, flids, kiddies, old biddies, pregnant birds or pussies.

SCENE TWO

The Waltzers. RAILTON *crushes* MELANIE *into the corner of a car. They shout over the music.*

RAILTON. I said you should've sat on this side.

MELANIE. I thought you wanted me to end up crushed.

RAILTON. Why would I wanna waste another quid-fifty?

MELANIE. If you try, you can pull back that way.

RAILTON. If I pull back we'll stop spinning. If I wanted a kids' ride I'd have gone on the dodgems.

MELANIE. What's wrong with the dodgems?

RAILTON. Nothing, for kids. No point when you've got a real car.

MELANIE. You can't ram people in a real car.

RAILTON. Can't you not?

MELANIE. Stop spinning it so much or I'll be sick on you.

RAILTON. No you won't. You'll be sick on them over there. Don't you know physics?

MELANIE. Stop spinning it, please.

RAILTON. It's the Waltzers. It's supposed to spin. Fuck's sake, why d'you pick it?

MELANIE. Cos it was on the ground. I thought it'd be safe.

RAILTON. You don't come here to be safe.

MELANIE. I'm going to be sick.

RAILTON. Why d'you come here?

> MELANIE *can't answer. Her hand is clapped over her mouth.* RAILTON *pushes the bar back and climbs out onto the moving platform. He holds out his hand. She shakes her head, terrified.*

Come on, blondie. I'll keep you safe. Trust me.

Blackout. Music continues.

SCENE THREE

Behind the arcade. The music and sounds of fruit machines and spilling cash are muffled. MELANIE *bends over, finishing up her heaving.* RAILTON *stands behind, lifting her plait.*

MELANIE (*wiping her mouth*). Don't look at me.

RAILTON. It smells worse if I shut me eyes.

MELANIE. Get lost.

> RAILTON *gives her a bottle of water. She takes it and drinks deep.*

RAILTON. Why d'you come here?

MELANIE. Cos there's nothing else to do. I've just got back and everyone's gone.

RAILTON. Everyone's not gone.

MELANIE. Everyone I knew has, except the people I don't want to know, and I'm not going to go out with my folks on a Friday night, am I?

RAILTON. Why d'you go away?

MELANIE. I went to London, to uni, then I've been travelling, round India and Tibet. I'm meant to be in Mexico.

RAILTON. Why I said, not where. *Why* d'you go?

MELANIE. I told you. To uni.

RAILTON. You can do degrees here, at the college.

MELANIE. I know, but come on.

RAILTON. What? Was there not nothing to do in London? Did you know everyone there?

MELANIE. There was so much to do that you could just do nothing. And nobody knew you. That was the best bit . . . D'you know what? If I went in a shop often enough that they started saying 'Hello' and 'The usual?', I stopped going there and went somewhere else. You can't do that here. You go into a shop and they all went to school with you or something hideous and they all talk like they know you even if they don't. That's why I came here. With all the lights and the crowds, you can pretend like it's Piccadilly Circus. You can lose yourself.

RAILTON. Till I screwed it up by finding you.

MELANIE. That's alright, Batman. I don't know you, do I . . . (*worried*) . . . I don't, do I? What school did you go to?

RAILTON. Not yours, don't worry.

MELANIE. What's your name?

RAILTON. Best stick with Batman, eh? Don't wanna scare you off.

MELANIE. And why are you here on your own, Batman?

RAILTON. Cos I always came to the fairs with my dad, but now he's dead.

MELANIE. Oh. I'm sorry.

RAILTON. S'alright. Shouldn't be going out with my folks on a Friday night, should I?

MELANIE. I never meant –

RAILTON. But it's alright cos I don't feel like I'm on my own cos I know everyone, and cos they all talk to me whether they know me or not, and cos there's loads to do. There's more to do than in Piccadilly Circus, which int even a circus. It's just a fucking road, and a crap one at that. You ever tried driving through it? . . . Don't bother. It's worse than the dodgems.

MELANIE (*pause*). D'you wanna go on the dodgems?

RAILTON. Best not with your belly, eh blondie? Although I reckon you've got rid of everything in it.

MELANIE. Yeah. Hope so.

RAILTON. You alright?

MELANIE (*pause, smiles*). I'm starving.

Blackout. Music blasts back once more.

SCENE FOUR

A bench. The music fades into the distance. RAILTON *and*
MELANIE *huddle up with a cone of chips and a spliff.*
MELANIE *sniffs the chips.*

MELANIE. I think they're cooked in animal fat. I can't eat
them.

RAILTON. You wanted them. I can't eat them.

MELANIE. Are you a veggie too?

RAILTON. I'm an anti-veggie. I don't eat veg.

MELANIE. That's stupid.

RAILTON. My sister works in a factory where they make veg,
cutting spuds into chips and carrots into strips and caulies
into florets for poncey restaurants and them rip-off bags in
supermarkets, Vegetable Medleys. She does twelve-hour
shifts and comes back brain dead and coated in stinking
starch. So I'm boycotting veg on principle. Cruelty to
humans. How many humans have gone mad for that cone of
chips?

MELANIE. So why d'you buy it?

RAILTON. Cos you said you were starving. Almost a fiver I've
wasted on you now.

MELANIE. I'm sorry. I am starving.

RAILTON (*pause*). Tell you what, why don't you come back
to mine?

MELANIE (*pause*). I don't know.

RAILTON. Why not?

MELANIE. I don't know you.

RAILTON. That's the best bit, int it? . . . Go on. It's only over the road. I've got a bong ready for blast off and we can stop at the shop for some munchies. Don't worry, I'll make sure the shopkeeper won't talk to you.

MELANIE (*giggles*). You promise?

RAILTON. You can't understand owt he says anyway.

MELANIE (*covers giggles with her hand*). You can't say that.

RAILTON. I can walk you back to yours if you'd rather. Would you rather go home?

Blackout. The fair music fades away.

SCENE FIVE

RAILTON*'s house. The settee is a Waltzer car, strewn with papers.* RAILTON *runs in to tidy and put on some music – the R&B tune that was last playing in the background.* MELANIE *enters.*

MELANIE. Get lost!

RAILTON (*looking round, uptight*). What?

MELANIE. That's unreal. Is that your sofa?

RAILTON. Oh, me settee. Yeah. It's mine now, I suppose.

He goes off into the kitchen. She looks around.

MELANIE. This place'd be worth a bomb somewhere else, you know?

RAILTON. I know.

MELANIE. I just mean, it's cool, having a whole house to yourself.

RAILTON. Not really.

MELANIE. Shit. Sorry . . . What happened to your dad, if you don't mind talking about it?

He re-enters before she can poke around too much and hands her a can.

RAILTON. I don't mind, but you might. Why don't you sit

down and talk while I fix us up? (*He goes off again, she sits and sips in silence.*) Tell us why you left.

MELANIE. I've told you, to go to –

RAILTON. Uni blah blah blah. But after that. Why d'you go to Mexico?

MELANIE. I never got to fucking Mexico, did I? (*Slumps back and swigs.*) The bastard dumped me in Tibet.

RAILTON. Shit. Sorry.

MELANIE. I don't care.

RAILTON. Good.

MELANIE. He's a bastard.

RAILTON. Fuck him. Move on.

MELANIE. He'll be out there in Mexico right now, living it up at the Day of the Dead, while I'm stuck here with the living dead.

RAILTON (*enters with a Coke bottle bong which he lifts in a toast*). Cheers.

MELANIE. I don't mean you, I just –

RAILTON. I know what you mean. (*Sits with her.*) Here. Have a go on this, chill out.

They both take blasts on the bong. RAILTON *holds his breath while* MELANIE *continues.*

MELANIE. No, I mean. Imagine. Coming straight back here from Tibet. From the top of the world to its pits. Right back to my single bed in my little pink bedroom –

RAILTON (*exhales, grinning*). Imagine.

MELANIE. – as if I'd never left. Except that now I've got a job.

RAILTON. That's summat then.

MELANIE. Oh yeah, just what I had planned.

RAILTON. Not at the spud factory are you?

MELANIE. Sorry. I must sound like a spoilt bitch.

RAILTON. Not a bitch.

MELANIE. I'm not spoilt. Dad gives me all the shit jobs just to prove it.

RAILTON. Dad put me on extrusion. I climbed out the bog window on my first shift.

MELANIE. Would you rather be a student and community liaison officer?

RAILTON. Dunno. Depends what one is.

MELANIE. One is one of me, innit? (*Fixed grin, chirpy voice.*) Can I help you, sir?

RAILTON. I can see two of you now.

MELANIE (*rubs her eyes*). I know what you mean. I think I'm really stoned.

RAILTON. You're not stoned enough then.

Blackout. The music fast-forwards to a slower track.

SCENE SIX

Later. They're slumped together, leaning in the corner of the settee.

MELANIE. Stop it spinning. You're making it spin.

RAILTON. Enjoy it. Here –

He reaches towards her. She flinches away, but he just pulls the elastic from her plait.

Let it dangle. (*She shakes out her hair.*) Int that better?

MELANIE. You tell me, Batman. Or should I say . . . Bruce Wayne!

Laughing, she unmasks him, pulling off his cap and throwing it in the air. His head is shaved.

Woah. That's hardcore. You're not a Nazi are you?

RAILTON. Nah, I'm a ginger. Don't tell anyone.

MELANIE. I won't if you won't. I'm one too, deep down. (*He glances at her lap. She giggles.*) I didn't mean –

RAILTON. Don't worry, you'll always be blondie to me. We'll have more fun that way, eh?

MELANIE. I am having fun. It's weird. I haven't been to a fair for years till tonight. I'd forgotten what it was like.

RAILTON. I've been to every single one down there since all I could do was play with the prizes. Couldn't shift in my cot for cuddly toys.

MELANIE. I won a prize, the last time I went.

RAILTON. Funny you stopped going then.

MELANIE. It's not funny. It's horrible. I won a goldfish.

RAILTON. You should see my bedroom. It's like 'Finding bleeding Nemo' up there. You still got yours?

MELANIE (*shakes her head, pause*). As soon as I won it, I took it down to the river and . . .

RAILTON. You gonna break my heart, blondie?

MELANIE. I didn't take it to the river to set it free. I took it there so no one could see me. My folks were back in the car, parked up, safe with their newspapers and flask. I made a hole in the plastic bag with my nail, and I squeezed it till all the water drained out. Dad had told me they only had five-second memories so I didn't think it'd feel anything, but watching it, blinking and gasping with the plastic shrinking tight to it . . . (*Wells up with tears.*) Shit, sorry. Do you hate me?

RAILTON (*bursts out laughing*). Don't be daft.

MELANIE. It's not funny.

RAILTON. It's a fucking fish.

MELANIE. I haven't eaten fish since. Or set foot in a fairground.

RAILTON. You're alright, it's safe now. There must've been a rash of fish massacres cos you just win fish-shaped jelly babies these days.

MELANIE. It's not safe. Couldn't you smell the danger tonight? All those pissed-up blokes picking fights. It's bad after the riots.

RAILTON. 'What a hell for eyes and ears! What anarchy and din barbarian and infernal! Tis a dream. Buffoons against

buffoons, grimacing, writhing, screaming. All freaks of
Nature, all Promethean thoughts of Man; his dullness,
madness, and their feats, all jumbled up together to make up
this Parliament of Monsters.'

MELANIE. What's that?

RAILTON. It's a fair.

MELANIE. It sounds like the riots.

RAILTON. It's poetry. Wordsworth, int it? My dad knew it by
heart.

MELANIE. He sounds like my dad. 'A little learning is a
dangerous thing; Drink deep, or taste not the Pierian spring.'

RAILTON. You want some of this spliff or are you stoned
enough yet?

MELANIE. Yeah . . . No . . . I don't know. Does that mean I am?

RAILTON. How's the spinning?

MELANIE. Pretty bad.

RAILTON. Maybe you should lean into me.

*She reaches towards him. He flinches away but she just
gently touches the back of his scalp.*

MELANIE. You've cut yourself shaving.

RAILTON. My dad used to do the back for me. I'm crap on
my own.

MELANIE. Does it hurt?

RAILTON. You could do it for me if you like. You could dye
it. Make me Mr Blonde, eh? . . . (*Sees she's welled up
again*). Here, it's not that bad, is it?

MELANIE. I'm still crying about that bastard fish. (*Wiping her
eyes.*) Don't look at me.

RAILTON. Don't cry, blondie. Chill out. Here.

*He holds out the spliff. She goes to take it but he moves it
away from her fingers.*

Close your eyes. Hold on.

*She closes her eyes and opens her mouth. He kisses her. She
holds onto him. Blackout.*

SCENE SEVEN

Later. The room is dark and silent, then traditional fairground
music chimes softly and the lights rise to a dim glow.
GEORGE *stands wearing a sheet with ghost eye and mouth*
holes cut out. He holds a book. The only bits of him showing
are his big tattooed arms, pyjama bottoms and slippers.
RAILTON *enters in his pyjama bottoms, barefoot. He grins,*
and whispers the sound of a ghost-train track rising.

RAILTON. Click . . . click . . . click . . . BOO! (GEORGE
drops the book.) Did I scare you?

GEORGE. Did you fuck.

> *They both pat their pyjama pockets.* GEORGE *pulls out a*
> *fag.* RAILTON *pulls out a spliff. They spark up*
> *simultaneously.*

RAILTON. What you up to?

GEORGE (*picks up book, clears throat and reads*). 'Pepper's
Ghost. To achieve this pop-lear showman's illusion, place
the mirror at an angle at the front of the stage, (*Nods at*
audience.) stand at the side, clad in ghost costume, and
position the projector thus. A modicum of smoke will
enhance the e-thereal effect.' (*Coughs out fag smoke.*)

RAILTON. Very ethereal.

GEORGE. Just you wait. It's going to be great. How's your
stuff coming along?

RAILTON. I met a girl at the fair tonight.

GEORGE (*takes off his sheet, he is smiling*). I met your
mother at the fair.

RAILTON. I know. / Side by side on the Super Speedway,
'Ticket to Ride' rocking round you /

GEORGE. / Side by side on the Super Speedway, 'Ticket to
Ride' rocking round us / Ride of me life. Won us a party
packet of Lucky Strikes on the Hook-a-Duck and we
smoked 'em all in one go. Struck well lucky for once.

RAILTON (*hits punchbag hard, a bell zings*). Me too. Heart's
banging too fast to sleep.

GEORGE. From round here, is she?

RAILTON. Yeah, sort of.

GEORGE. Do I know her?

RAILTON. She's been in London.

GEORGE. Don't you go getting distracted, you've got stuff to do. Important stuff.

RAILTON. We was side by side on the Revolution, 'Dutty Rock' rocking round us.

GEORGE. Bloody techno rubbish I bet.

RAILTON. S'not techno, s'ragga. Get with it, old man.

GEORGE. Fucking ragga. Not having none of that I hope.

RAILTON. Nah, course not.

GEORGE. And lay off that ganja crap, an all. Got to stay focused, don't we?

RAILTON. I know.

GEORGE. Don't let me down, son.

RAILTON. I won't. I promise.

GEORGE. Good lad . . . Go and fix that mirror for us, will you? Can't get the angle right for the life of me.

RAILTON *comes right up to the audience. He turns and looks back at* GEORGE. *They both drop their smokes simultaneously.* GEORGE *crushes his under his slipper.* RAILTON *goes to crush his barefoot and yelps.* GEORGE *laughs.*

S'what I mean. Got to stay alert, Railton, else you'll get hurt.

Blackout.

SCENE EIGHT

The college hall. Silence. MELANIE, *wearing a sarong, T-shirt and trainers, enters with a clipboard, mobile and pile of papers which she puts down to clear up the set. She acknowledges the audience occasionally with a fixed smile, then finally by speaking.*

MELANIE. Thank you for your patience, we should be getting started any minute now . . . If you haven't already done so, could you please take a moment to check that your mobiles and pagers are turned off? Thanks . . . Um, I believe there was a mix-up with the photocopying, but don't worry if you didn't get the 'Fair' section of the community-cohesion strategy. The, um, principal will recap when he gets here and I've got some multilingual versions . . . somewhere . . . *(As she juggles her papers, a hip-hop polyphonic ringtone begins to plink, she drops the papers.)* Shit. Sorry. I mean, Christ, sugar, is that . . . ? I think that's me. Sorry. Excuse me . . . *(Answers phone and mutters.)* Hello? . . . Oh . . . No . . . No . . . No. That's not . . . But . . . *(Hangs up, smiles.)* I'm afraid Mr Bradshaw's been held up in a board meeting. He says we should get started without him. Um . . .

RAILTON *enters, wearing a suit and carrying a briefcase.*

RAILTON. Sorry I'm late –

MELANIE. That's okay, take a . . .

They recognise each other and stop dead in their tracks.

Can I help you, sir?

RAILTON. Yeah . . . I reckon / I might be in the wrong place. /

MELANIE. / You might be in the wrong place. / *(To audience.)* Excuse me a second . . . Excuse us.

She hurries with him out of the hall, where they have a tumbling, hushed, blushing exchange. The shift from inside the hall and out, can be indicated by a lighting change.

RAILTON. What're you doing here?

MELANIE. You never said you worked here.

RAILTON. I don't call it work. Fucking student, aren't I?

MELANIE. Are you?

RAILTON. Suppose I do go to your school, sort of.

MELANIE. You don't look like a student.

RAILTON. Don't you like it?

MELANIE. No. I mean yeah, I do. You look nice.

RAILTON. Blown my dealing profits on my degree so I reckoned I should do it properly.

MELANIE. I hardly recognised you.

RAILTON. Cheers.

MELANIE. In your clothes, those clothes, I mean. I mean –

RAILTON. I know what you mean.

MELANIE. Shit. Did I slag off doing degrees here? I didn't mean it.

RAILTON. I thought you did.

MELANIE. I should keep my big trap shut.

RAILTON. Dunno about that, blondie . . .

Pause.

MELANIE. / I'm sorry I – /

RAILTON. / You didn't have to / sneak off. You could've woke me up, you know.

MELANIE. I know. I wanted to. Wake you, not sneak off. I just didn't want to wake you.

RAILTON. I looked for you down the fair on Saturday.

MELANIE. They dragged me to see my bloody granddad.

RAILTON. You don't have to say that.

MELANIE. It's true. I sulked all day.

RAILTON. Me too. When I weren't grinning.

MELANIE. I went back down there on Sunday but –

RAILTON. It'd moved on. Snuck off in the night.

MELANIE. It looked like a battleground, with all the litter.

RAILTON. Thought I'd lost you, blondie.

MELANIE. I kept smelling your aftershave on my hair.

RAILTON. Sorry.

MELANIE. I didn't want to wash it out.

RAILTON. I won you these. (*Pulls a paperbag from his pocket.*)
Veggie-friendly goldfish. Just jellybabies really, but –

MELANIE (*takes them*). That's really sweet. Thanks.

RAILTON. I was going to come and find you. I didn't know
you'd be here.

MELANIE. Can I meet you afterwards? I won't be long.

RAILTON. What're you doing here?

MELANIE. Running this bloody community meeting. My
dad's dropped me right in it.

RAILTON. Oh. / You're not stopping, are you? I've got to. /

MELANIE. / You're not coming, are you? I've got to. / Oh.

RAILTON. / Who's your dad? /

MELANIE. / What community / are you representing,
Batman? Local heroes?

RAILTON (*pause*). Can I meet you afterwards?

MELANIE. Yeah, course you can.

RAILTON. Whatever happens?

MELANIE. What do you mean?

RAILTON (*kisses her*). Just remember, you like me, don't you?

MELANIE. What? (*Checks clipboard.*) What's your name?
What's your . . . ?

RAILTON *has re-entered the hall. He takes a seat in the
audience.* MELANIE *takes centre stage.*

For those of you who don't . . . know me, my name's
Melanie Bradshaw, as in Principal Bradshaw, but I'm sure
you won't hold that against me, will you? (*Smiles, sorts
through papers.*) So. I'll just read a little from his notes to
set the scene and then I'll hand over to you, because this is
your fair, and I'm just here to, um, facilitate your vision.
(*Finding paper.*) Hold on. Where are we? Here we go. Here
we go. Okay, so he says: (*Reads.*) 'A Fair for the Future.'
(*Clears throat.*) 'One year on from the race-related distur-
bances that highlighted problems of deep polarisation and
fragmented communities living parallel lives in the town, a

number of solutions have been identified by an independent
scrutiny' . . . um, time's quite tight, so let me just find the
bit about the actual fair . . . Here we go . . . 'This landmark
event will be a fair for everyone, a fair for the future that will
help us to establish a common vision and sense of belonging.
National identity is not an antique. It is a shared dream that
we have to constantly reimagine. We need to reimagine our
past and create a future that includes us all.' . . . So! That's
all we have to do in the next hour or so. (*Smiles.*) Let's hear
what you've come up with. (*Checks list.*) Aftab Amjad from
oh, FAIR, cool, that's the Forum Against Islamophobia and
Racism . . . oh, cool, he's sent in a written submission, so . . .
Okay, Railton Hills from another group called FAIR. It
doesn't say what it stands for.

RAILTON (*stands up*). Fighting Anti-white Racism.

MELANIE. Oh. You're Railton.

RAILTON. Yeah. (*Takes papers from his briefcase.*) Do you
mind?

MELANIE. I don't know. Time's quite –

RAILTON. Tight. I know. I won't be long . . . Hullo everyone.
I should kick off by saying that yeah, I am George Hills's
son, which you might well hold against me, but that's your
problem. And whilst we're getting things straight, this int
your fair, it's his. He knew this town, he knew the people
from here and he knew fairs better than anyone, and he
loved 'em all. I've been going through some of his stuff . . .
wait up, give us a chance. Before you knew his name from
the papers, you might've seen him in the town centre with
his carousel for kids what he built himself. Or if you're
interested in history what's not on the syllabus, you
might've seen him down the historical society giving talks
on fairs. No? Well, you don't know everything, do you?
Like I bet you never knew that there was a fair here before
there was even a town, did you? Listen. In 1204, a charter
was granted to hold a fair in this borough, but that was only
when the king got his finger out, red tape being just as crap
back then. The fair had already been going for years. Right
here. Bringing people together, a day away from the grind
to celebrate being part of summat. That's how this
community started. That's what we've forgotten. I know

we've been told our past is summat to be ashamed of, but I'm not ashamed of my forefathers. Course our national identity's not an antique cos we've flogged it for whatever's in this season. Ethnic throws or an Ikea sofa, that's all we're supposed to fight for now. We need to go back to what we know, not forward into God knows what future. My dad's dream was to hold a fair here that made people proud of themselves again. A proper English fair, held on St George's Day, for all the forgotten, honest, hard-working people, the majority of the people in this town. I can see you all wanting me to shut up and piss off spoiling your fun, but that's just what'll turn this fair into another landmark riot, and it was a riot, though it'll look like a disturbance compared to what'll happen if you hijack us cash for your vision. So get real and facilitate this. This is our town and our fair. We paid for it. Dad paid for it, dearly, and I'm going to make his dream come true.

Blackout.

SCENE NINE

College hall, later. MELANIE *is leaving.* RAILTON, *waiting at the door, blocks her.*

RAILTON. I'm wide awake now, Mel. No need to sneak off.

MELANIE. Get out of my way.

RAILTON. You said you'd meet us.

MELANIE. I didn't know –

RAILTON. What?

MELANIE. Who you were.

RAILTON. Who am I?

MELANIE. You know.

RAILTON. Yeah, I do, and I know you like me.

MELANIE. If I knew you were a racist thug I'd never have . . .

RAILTON. What?

MELANIE. Spoken to you.

RAILTON. But you did speak to me. Several times. Just give us a chance, will you?

MELANIE. No, just go.

RAILTON. Go where? London? India? Tibet? I come here. I don't want to go anywhere else.

MELANIE. Let me go then. I'm busy.

RAILTON. Let me help you then.

MELANIE. No thanks.

RAILTON. Hear us out at least.

MELANIE. I've heard plenty already.

She pushes past him, dropping the bag of sweets.

RAILTON. Hold up, you've dropped your –

MELANIE. I can't eat them. Gelatine.

She goes. He puts one of the sweets in his mouth and then spits it out and sits down, head in his hands. The lights go down and then back up again. Later. He's still there. MELANIE *enters, loaded up with files. She stops in her tracks when she sees him.*

What are you doing here?

RAILTON. Waiting for you.

MELANIE. Have you been here all day?

RAILTON. I'm dying for a piss.

MELANIE. So go for a piss then.

He doesn't move. MELANIE *looks around.*

RAILTON. It's alright. It's your job to liaise with me, int it?

MELANIE. Not for long. They will kick you out, you know.

RAILTON. They can't. They've no right to. And neither have you. It'll take more than shampoo to get rid of me.

MELANIE. I knew I shouldn't have gone on that bloody ride.

RAILTON. Well, you're strapped in now so you're stuck with me. You can't reimagine your past so's I don't exist and you can't keep running away. I won't let you.

MELANIE. How will you stop me? Torch my house? Start a riot?

RAILTON. Buy you a pint. Roll you a spliff. Talk to you. Come on, blondie.

MELANIE. Don't call me that.

RAILTON (*loudly*). Madam Chair, I request an urgent dialogue by the rights of the unwritten contract of fucking good manners between two people who've –

MELANIE. Keep your voice down, will you?

RAILTON. No. I won't. Not till you've let me explain.

MELANIE. I'm not listening to racist shit.

RAILTON. You're not listening at all. I'm not a racist thug no more than you're a spoilt bitch, so give me a chance. Give us a chance, Melanie.

MELANIE (*pause*). I don't know.

RAILTON. You don't wanna go home, do you?

MELANIE. I don't want to be here.

RAILTON. I know somewhere no one'll see us.

Blackout.

SCENE TEN

The hill at dusk. RAILTON has his back turned, finishing a piss. Beside him on the floor is a corner-shop carrier bag. MELANIE puts down her small rucksack and inspects her trainers.

MELANIE. I'm covered in cow shit.

RAILTON (*relieved sigh, zipping up*). Watch out for the new reservoir there. Done my bit to combat global warming I reckon.

MELANIE. It's bloody freezing up here.

RAILTON. Did your bloke dump you up a mountain for whinging or summat?

MELANIE. No, he didn't.

RAILTON. I didn't mean it like that. (*Takes his jacket off and offers it to her.*) I just meant, I thought you liked travelling.

MELANIE. I like going somewhere (*Takes jacket, holds it.*)

RAILTON. This is somewhere . . . Don't you think it's beautiful?

MELANIE. Suppose so, in a bleak kind of way. (*Puts jacket on.*) It's not Tibet.

RAILTON. Thank fuck for that.

MELANIE. Here we go.

RAILTON. No, I just mean, there's nowhere like it in the world. (*Climbing up on the scaffold and looking out.*) Even a few miles away, the moors leave me cold. It's like I've got this homing signal, a big fuck-off pigeon flapping in me guts when this big-dipper hillside rears up and you look down on it all. Helter-skelter chimneys. Amazing maze of terraced streets and canals. Massive stripy sky, all funhouse sunset . . . Whereabouts is your house?

MELANIE. I don't know.

RAILTON. Don't worry, I won't torch it.

MELANIE. No, I mean, I'm not sure where it is exactly . . . (*Climbs up too and points it out*). It's there I think, by the trees.

RAILTON. Very nice.

MELANIE. It's not my house anyway.

RAILTON *takes a picnic – a tube of Pringles and two cans of White Lightning – from his bag. He offers a can to her.*

I told you, I'm not getting pissed with you. Didn't you get me some water?

RAILTON (*hands her a bottle of water*). Yeah, some Pierian Spring. Drink deep.

MELANIE. What?

RAILTON. Forget it. (*Watches her.*) You can't wait to go, can you?

MELANIE (*checks watch*). I said I'd give you till dinner . . . tea.

RAILTON. Away, I mean. Somewhere.

MELANIE. Suppose I'll have to stay till the fair's finished.

RAILTON. Have your bit of fun and fuck off again like all the rest, eh?

MELANIE. It's just a fair, Railton. It doesn't matter.

RAILTON. I know this is just a holiday job, a holiday fling for you, but some of us live here.

MELANIE. We all live here. See that big grey thing there? It's called a motorway. And your stripes in the sky? Aeroplanes made them.

RAILTON. Sorry, blondie, but your global-community bollocks means fuck all when you can't afford a fortnight in Falaraki.

MELANIE. That's not what this is about.

RAILTON. Course it is. It's all about cash, int it? This is what I mean. I'm not racist. The problem isn't cohesive fucking blah blah blah. The problem's simple. We pay top dollar for the shittest health, housing, schools and you name it cos your government –

MELANIE. It's not my government.

RAILTON. – wants its global economy so we have to give up everything and whatever's left gets diverted to your diverse mates –

MELANIE. To who?

RAILTON. You know, to your asylum seekers and –

MELANIE. Yeah, that's what this is about and it's a load of crap. There's hardly any asylum seekers here –

RAILTON. You know who to thank for that –

MELANIE. – there never were, it's all bullshit, and those there are are hardly rolling in it.

RAILTON. No, you don't understand.

MELANIE. No I don't. They belong here as much as we do.

RAILTON. What do you know about belonging?

MELANIE. I know history 'what is' on the syllabus. I know people have always come here.

RAILTON. You know what they wanted you to know. Yeah, they've always come here, but we never bent over, we called 'em invasions and we fought for what we stood for. Things don't just fragment, Melanie. Someone's got to smash them. So now they're in bits and what do you stand for? You don't even know who you are. What are you?

MELANIE. What am I?

RAILTON. You might well ask. Northerner? Londoner? English? British? European? Westerner? Earthling? Some liberal pick 'n' mix bag of this week's bits 'n' shits with nice new Nikes and a sprinkling of new-age guff from Madonna? Some American fucking dream that's the last thing we want to follow?

MELANIE. What are you?

RAILTON. A White Briton apparently. And what the fuck is that?

MELANIE. If it's you, I'd rather not be one. I'm not anything, Railton. I'm just me.

RAILTON. Yeah, me me me. You sulk cos you have to come back here and do summat. You sulk cos you have to see your granddad once in a blue moon cos you're too busy running round trying to lose yourself or find yourself and you know what? You're already lost, cos you've fallen for their spiel. You've forgotten what's real. Like all the rest, getting out of town if they can and out of their heads if they can't. You think your fair's gonna help them? It'll freak 'em out even more, poor fuckers. It's the last straw. (*Lights spliff with shaking hands.*) It has to matter, Mel, or nothing matters.

MELANIE (*pause*). Listen, Railton. I understand.

RAILTON. Do you?

MELANIE. Yeah, but you're wrong. It's not me that's mixed up. There is no us and them. You didn't grow up out of the mud here, however much you mark out your territory.

That's not a pigeon in your guts. It's just fear. That's all I'm hearing, and there's nothing to be scared of. It can be great. Listen, when I was in London, I used to get the tube every morning with people of every race, all getting on together –

RAILTON. That's not the point.

MELANIE. It is. Listen –

RAILTON. The point is the tube's shit. Don't matter if it had Martians sitting next to you playing three-eyed 'I Spy', it'd still be a rip-off and break down every other fucking day, wouldn't it?

MELANIE. Yeah, but –

RAILTON. I know no one can be arsed to speak to each other on the tube but I bet if they did they won't be singing 'I'd like to buy the world a fucking Coke'. Get on a bus here and see if people feel like part of a big happy family or if they feel like the world's fucked 'em off. But of course you won't cos you know what's best and you don't give a shit what they actually think.

MELANIE. You don't know. My dad can't fart without having a public consultation first.

RAILTON. Fuck consultations and focus groups and Appendix Y for any other comments. I don't want a pie chart, I want my rightful fucking slice.

MELANIE. Why do you think I came up here?

RAILTON. Cos you like me.

MELANIE. No.

RAILTON. For a quick fuck with a bit of rough?

MELANIE. To give you a chance, to talk to you . . . I have to believe you can change.

RAILTON. Can you?

MELANIE. What?

RAILTON. Change.

MELANIE. Course I can.

RAILTON. What to? Tory?

MELANIE. Fuck off.

RAILTON. What can you change to when you've no choice?

MELANIE. I know but –

RAILTON. No, but what if it really matters?

MELANIE. Then you wouldn't pick the BNP. They won't make it any better.

RAILTON. I dunno, I've already done pretty well for myself, don't you think? How else d'you reckon I'd have a say at that meeting today? Couldn't bank on going out with the principal's daughter.

MELANIE. We're not going –

RAILTON. No, you see? No one else wants us. School kicked us out. Work laid us off, me and my dad. None of the other parties was bothered about doing owt except bleating the same bollocks and bitching at each other, trying to prove there's a papercut of difference between 'em. The BNP gave us a chance to win more than just a cuddly toy, so we snatched it. My dad ran their FAIR campaign.

MELANIE. So the name was his big idea. I couldn't figure it out.

RAILTON. It's an anachronism, int it? Fighting Anti-white Racism.

MELANIE. You mean an acronym, I think. But it doesn't spell 'fair' anyway.

RAILTON. Sorry he wasn't the fucking principal. He didn't run a branding exercise first. He just wanted to get stuff done. And he did. He did well. He listened to people, instead of just shoving shiny happy multicultural bullshit like pizza leaflets through their doors. So they put him up for the council. And then it got really good. We campaigned together. Two fingers up to them who said I'd never come to nothing. (GEORGE *enters in a monster mask and climbs up the scaffold to the top.*) Check us out, centre stage, in front of the crowds, all cheering us on . . . it was like heaven. For a second. Then a gang of Pakis torched the lock-up where he kept his carousel. They might as well have stabbed him in the heart, but they're too pussy for that, eh? Just a heart attack, the pigs said. No one's fault. No one gave a shit. How's that fucking fair?

MELANIE. I don't know. (*Takes his hand.*) I'm sorry, Railton.
But fighting won't help.

RAILTON. He held me hand . . . He was staring at me so hard,
like he was trying to tell us summat. Tell us to keep going.
To never forget. To get the bastards back.

MELANIE. Maybe he wasn't. Maybe he was trying to tell you
he'd been wrong.

RAILTON *looks at her, then goes to kiss her. She pulls
away.*

RAILTON. Why not? You still like us, don't you?

MELANIE. No. I don't know. I think I understand but then
you let something evil slip. You say something ugly like . . .

RAILTON. What?

MELANIE. You know what –

RAILTON. It is ugly. Listen. Paki-paki-paki-paki. Look at it.
(*Grabs her head and forces her to look outwards.*) It looks
pretty from a distance but look at it in close-up: the
chimneys're falling down, the canal's swimming with filth
and the streets aren't safe to walk down. The world's an
ugly place, Melanie Bradshaw. Whatever you can and can't
say. Or will or won't say.

MELANIE. Fuck you. Get off me.

RAILTON. What if you can't get away?

MELANIE. I'll scream.

RAILTON. So scream. (*He screams.*) I used to scream up here
all the time. No one hears. That's why I joined the BNP.
D'you understand now?

MELANIE. Get your fucking Neanderthal hands off me.

RAILTON. That's better, let's have a real dialogue. You hate
'em too, don't you?

MELANIE. No, I hate you.

RAILTON. See them trees where your big houses are? That's
where they voted my dad in. Where all the pretty people
who whisper 'Paki' live. Who did your dad vote for?

MELANIE. Not for your dad. Get off me.

RAILTON. How do you know what he spits in his head when he sits through another consultation? Don't you think in the polling booth he might just've let rip?

MELANIE (*yanks her head away*). He votes fucking Tory if you must know, only no Tories bothered standing. And my mum doesn't vote at all.

RAILTON. And what about you?

MELANIE. I wasn't here.

RAILTON. So the Bradshaws can sleep sound in the knowledge that they never did nowt.

MELANIE. I don't know who I'd vote for but it'd never be you. Your dad's dead and so's his world, Railton. Move on.

She tries to go. He grabs her, but she squirms out of the jacket until it's empty in his fist.

RAILTON. Don't go. Where are you going?

MELANIE. Stay away from me, Railton. Don't come near me again. (*Exits.*)

RAILTON. You don't mean that . . . I didn't mean to . . . Come back . . . Fuck it!

He throws the jacket down into the mud and stamps on it. Finally, he sits, exhausted, and sparks up. The lights dim. At the back, GEORGE *climbs down, making the ghost-train sound.*

GEORGE. Click . . . click . . . click . . . BOO! (RAILTON *jumps,* GEORGE *laughs.*) Got you that time, didn't I? (*Sniffs the air.*) You proper shit yourself.

RAILTON. No I never.

GEORGE. D'you remember you was little and I took you on the ghost train?

RAILTON. Course I remember.

GEORGE. I wound you up summat rotten before we'd even set off and you were shitting yerself in the car, holding me hand that tight you almost broke me bones.

RAILTON. D'you remember when you held my hand?

GEORGE. I was just playing along with you, having you on.

RAILTON. No, not then. When you . . . wanted to tell us summat. Remember? What was it? Was you scared?

GEORGE. Not scared of nothing, me. (*Lights a fag.*) What's up with you? Not lost your bottle cos of that lass, have you?

RAILTON. No. Course not.

GEORGE. Don't fuck it up, son. Look at me. (*Takes mask off.*) I loved your mum, but if she hadn't stopped me, we'd of been out there now, a proper fairground family.

RAILTON. Cos of the boxing booths.

GEORGE. If you got a knock-out, you got to stay on with the fair for good. How good would that've been?

BOTH. Pretty fucking good.

GEORGE. I was up against this spade.

RAILTON. Black Bomber Harris versus Georgie Kid Hills.

GEORGE (*shadow-boxing*). Crowd was roaring for the local lad, but he was slippery that spade, landed a few jabs before the bell, bust me bloody nose. I'd of had him, except your mum went mad. Saw the blood and started screaming for 'em to stop the fight. Put me right off and before I knew it, the black bastard had floored me. I was gonna go back next year and show him what for, but just my luck, the booths got banned. We didn't like fighting no more.

BOTH. Yeah right.

GEORGE. We just took it outside. Took off us gloves. You don't wanna be a loser, son, take it from me.

RAILTON. I'm not a loser.

GEORGE. I told her. I could of been the strongman and you could of been the fat lass.

RAILTON. She said it'd be living like pikeys.

GEORGE. I said it's purer blood than Buckingham Palace. Full-on family land, closer knit than bootees. But she wanted to play it safe and stay put. We got stuck. At the arse end of a waiting list, in a house worth less than a caravan.

RAILTON. I want to do summat, Dad.

GEORGE. Good lad. Can't just sit back and do nothing. Reckon on it's all okay when it int. Look at your mum. She weren't the fat lass no more, was she?

RAILTON. She kept saying, weren't her diet working well?

GEORGE. Human skellington more like. She'd of been perfect for the fair. Giving it the spiel.

BOTH. It's not the show. It's the tale you told.

RAILTON. Tom Norman the Silver King.

GEORGE. Master of the art of spiel. His words could slip into your pockets like a footpad's fingers, take your wage and take you through the dark, telling you you were seeing wonders when all it was was bits 'n' shits. Take note, our kid. There's showmen everywhere, telling you things are one way so you can't see what's real. Don't let her wind you up and blind you. Don't fuck it up, son.

RAILTON. I know, I won't, but sometimes . . .

GEORGE. What?

RAILTON. I dunno, it's hard to see in the dark.

GEORGE. Are you scared, Railton Hills?

RAILTON. No.

GEORGE (*puts fag out*). So prove it to me. (*Starts sparring.*) Come on, Rocket Railton. Show us your stuff. Are you gonna lose to a lass? To the Pakis?

RAILTON. No, but –

GEORGE. This is the last battle. You gonna lose at the last minute cos you're in love?

RAILTON. No. (*He hits out,* GEORGE *ducks and laughs and lands one on* RAILTON.)

GEORGE. Dropped your guard, didn't you? See what I mean? This int a love-in. This is a war. She'll blindside you if you let her, son. Trust me.

RAILTON. I do. (GEORGE *lands another.*)

GEORGE. Sure you've not gone soft? Sure you're not scared?

RAILTON. Am I fuck. (*He hits him and* GEORGE *reels back, clutching his chest.*) Shit, I'm sorry, are you alright? (*Goes to help him, but* GEORGE *moves away.*)

GEORGE. Course I am. (*Laughs, wheezing.*) Just having you on, aren't I? (*Puts mask on.*) Sort it out now, son, else you'll end up like me and no one'll give a shit.

RAILTON. I give a shit.

GEORGE. Prove it.

Blackout.

SCENE ELEVEN

College hall. MELANIE *enters with a big box and a bottle of water. She drinks deep and takes a moment to compose herself before turning around to face the audience.*

MELANIE. Morning everyone. I know it's an early start but there's a lot still to do and time's running out. The future's coming round fast . . . (*Smiles, stifles sickness.*) Thank you for your suggestions for the fair, which have all been taken on board, apart from those of our BNP representative who has regrettably just been suspended from the college and is under investigation for the sale of illegal substances on campus, so he won't be able to contribute to the project any longer. Perhaps it's for the best . . . (*Another swig and a smile.*) So, with that minor unpleasantness out of the way, let's get started on the good stuff.

She takes a large blank sheet of paper from the box and sticks it up at the back, then she gets a marker and writes 'A Fair for the Future' on the sheet in inexpert lettering. RAILTON *enters, pushing a double-pram. He watches her. A baby cries.*

(*Swings around at the sound.*) You're not allowed in here.

RAILTON. I had to pick their stuff up from the crèche. Thought I'd stop by and see what future you had in store for them . . . Not much, by the looks of things.

MELANIE. Will you take it outside, please?

RAILTON. Will you help me? Please?

MELANIE (*reluctantly, to the audience*). Excuse me a second.

They leave the hall. RAILTON *settles the baby with a dummy sweet till it's quiet.*

RAILTON. Beautiful, aren't they? You can hold one if you want.

MELANIE. No.

RAILTON. They're not contaminated.

MELANIE. You never told me you had –

RAILTON. They're not mine. They're my sister's. I look after them while she's working. I always brought 'em here while I was in lessons but now –

MELANIE. What do you want?

RAILTON. They're setting a new family record, getting kicked out at eighteen months.

MELANIE. I'm sorry.

RAILTON. Are you? So why d'you do it then?

MELANIE. You did it, didn't you?

RAILTON. How else am I meant to stump up for your crappy course? That's not why you grassed me up, is it?

MELANIE. I told you it was just a matter of time. There's no place here for racist thugs.

RAILTON. I'm not a fucking racist thug, are you deaf or daft or what?

MELANIE. You said 'Paki' and you hurt me. Racist. Thug.

RAILTON. Yeah, that's me. A racist thug drug-dealer who you hate. Believe what you want, blondie, but it won't change how things are. You can't get rid of me.

MELANIE. I have done, haven't I?

The baby starts crying again.

RAILTON. How's your baby coming along?

MELANIE. What?

RAILTON. The fair. (*Takes clipboard off her.*) This it then?

MELANIE. Give it back.

RAILTON. Poetry slam. Indian fashion show. Percussion workshop . . .

MELANIE. Don't take the piss.

RAILTON. I thought you were.

MELANIE. You're not coming to it, so it doesn't matter.

RAILTON. Oh right yeah, I see you've given the pigs an information tent on site. Watch out, they might recruit us to fight for them instead.

MELANIE. When will you learn, there's no point fighting?

RAILTON. Why not? (*Throws clipboard.*) Because you've already won? Cos I'm just a born fucking loser and I should get used to it and stop trying to do summat about it?

Both babies are crying now.

MELANIE. Shut them up, for fuck's sake. I can't stand it.

Pause. He stares at her, then closes his eyes and sniffs the air.

RAILTON. You feeling alright this morning, Melanie?

MELANIE. Go now or I'll call security.

RAILTON (*whispers*). Click . . . click . . . click . . .

MELANIE. Help! Someone!

RAILTON. Alright, alright, we're going. But we're not going far.

He goes. MELANIE *composes herself and goes back in.*

MELANIE. Sorry about that. Where was I? Oh yes. The future . . .

A soundtrack of different multicultural tunes kicks in as MELANIE *turns the poster around to reveal a poster for the fair.*

SCENE TWELVE

MELANIE *continues to set up the fair on the scaffold at the back using bits from her box, intermittently humming her tunes. In the foreground is* RAILTON*'s living room. He sits with his own box, taking out fairground models and showing them to the kids in the double-pram. He winds up one of the toys which plays a tinkling traditional fairground tune, like* GEORGE*'s ghost music.* RAILTON *talks to the kids in the pram.*

RAILTON. D'you know what this is? Granddad made it. It's the Learned Pig. No, not Principal Bradshaw. This un's from the eighteenth century when pigs performed all sorts of mad stuff for Blake and Coleridge and Dr Johnson, but forget about them, we're like, so over it, and there's no proper pigs near here anyway cos we've fucked up farming too, but no mind. What we got next? A haunted house! Plenty of them around here. We could use this whole street for free, couldn't we? No admission, just break in. Take home a prize if you're lucky and there's owt left. What's this? A carousel! Well, we could've had one of them, except some bastards torched it, but no mind, it's not their fault is it, and we can still go round and round in circles without a carousel here, can't we? Here we go. A Parliament of Monsters. Is it Westminster? Is it the town hall? No, it's a freak show! They should let one of them in, shouldn't they, if we call it summat PC, like Special Persons' Awareness Tent and pretend not to stare. Won't that be alright? No? How about a mirror maze then, so's they can see the real freaks staring back at 'em? How about a coconut shy? How about a boxing booth? How about a tribute to the Heart of England fairs where we just have an empty bit in the middle of the field? No? No? How did I know? I know what they'll like. How about candy floss? Candy fucking floss all round so no one'll even notice the shitty sideshows. (*The babies cry.* RAILTON *sniffs.*) What's that, babies? Yeah, I second that motion. (*Gets a nappy packet out from under the pram, and finds it empty.*) Sorry mate. You'll just have to live with it.

SCENE THIRTEEN

RAILTON *speaks to the BNP branch meeting through a mike like a fairground operator's. Simultaneously,* MELANIE *speaks to the fair action group through a megaphone.*

RAILTON. 'What need then, of fairs, and shows? The nation has outgrown them, and fairs are as dead as the generations which they have delighted, and the last showman will soon be as great a curiosity as the dodo.' That was written in 1870-summat but they've struggled on till now. And now my dad's the dodo and so are all of us. I never reckoned there'd be such dancing on his grave. He was trying to save us from this fete, but it's too late. They've wiped him out and kicked me out and fucked you all over all over again and there's nowt we can do about it. Unless we get organised and get everyone together. Give them a show they'll never forget. Are you with me? Are you ready? Let's go.

MELANIE. I'll admit it, I didn't want to come back here and I didn't want to do this job. All I'd heard about the town this last year was trouble and holding a fair on the anniversary of the riots seemed like a recipe for disaster, but I was wrong. Working with everyone, watching everything come together to create something out of nothing, something really special, has changed my mind. It's given me hope. If we can make this happen, we can do anything. It's not going to be easy. We've only a few days left and a 'To Do' list as long as this field, but if we get organised and keep working together, I know we can give them a show they'll never forget. Is everyone with me? Are you ready? Let's go.

The mixed-up traditional and multicultural music blasts out. Different coloured lights race in the darkness. In an echo of the opening scene, RAILTON *shaves his head while, beside him,* MELANIE *crouches, clutching a pregnancy test, eyes closed.* RAILTON *cuts his head. He touches it, smears blood across his scalp.* MELANIE *opens her eyes and looks down. Blackout. Silence.*

SCENE FOURTEEN

The river by the fairground. MELANIE *walks wearily down to the river, drinking from a bottle of water. She drops her clipboard, crouches down and washes her face. Then she takes the pregnancy test from her pocket, clutches it in her fist and stares at her reflection.*

MELANIE. We went to the Kumbh Fair in Varanasi, this massive festival where millions of Hindus go to bathe in the Ganges. Lepers go to get healed, pilgrims go to get saved, I went to get . . . I don't know. I didn't know what I wanted to do since uni and we weren't getting on. The trip was supposed to sort all that out, but it was making things worse. Everywhere we went did my head in. It all looked so beautiful to start with, but once you'd been there a day or two it didn't look so nice any more. There were so many sick people, beggars, poor little kids, grabbing my skirt, my bag, men staring at me. I felt like they hated me for being there, for being, I don't know. For being . . . me. I wasn't me. It didn't seem real. It was like I wasn't really there. I felt homesick. I don't know where for. I kept thinking I'd be alright in the next place, and the next and the next, but we never got there. Then we got to Varanasi and I thought, this is it. Something real will happen to me here. And it really fucking did. The river was full of crap from factories and it gave me the shits for weeks.

She is about to drop the little plastic stick in the water when RAILTON *enters. She stuffs her fist back in her pocket.*

RAILTON. Do you want us to hold your plait for you?

MELANIE. What do you want?

RAILTON. Fair's coming on up there. Almost ready for the off, eh?

MELANIE. What do you want?

RAILTON. I'm sorry about before.

MELANIE. Which bit?

RAILTON. All of it.

MELANIE. Yeah, me too.

RAILTON. No, it was alright to start with, wasn't it?

MELANIE. It was a mistake.

RAILTON. Don't say that. I don't want to lose you an all, blondie.

MELANIE. Well, bad luck, Railton, you have.

RAILTON. No, I've found you. Your action group's lost you. I knew you'd be down here. The scene of the crime.

MELANIE. What?

RAILTON. Your goldfish.

MELANIE. Oh. I forgot I told you that.

RAILTON. You can tell me stuff, Mel. Whatever you want. We can talk, us, can't we?

MELANIE. I don't want to talk to anyone.

RAILTON. You been crying?

MELANIE. It's just the river.

RAILTON. You're crying now.

MELANIE. That fucking fish.

She covers her face. He tries to comfort her. She fights him, pushing him away, then gives in.

RAILTON. It's alright, Mel. Everything'll be alright.

MELANIE. I'm meant to be in Mexico.

RAILTON. You're better off here, with your family, with me.

MELANIE. I hate this place, I hate my family, I hate you and I hate this fucking fair. I'm not having fun any more. My head's spinning.

She pulls out a fag packet and sparks up with shaking hands. RAILTON *takes the fag off her.*

RAILTON. Don't do that. Give it to me . . . I can help you. I'll look after it.

MELANIE. The fair?

RAILTON (*shakes his head, pause*). I went to the chemists to get some nappies for the kids. The chemists by the bus station, you know? . . . I know the lass who works there. Sheralyn Stack, d'you know her? . . . She knows you. She went to school with you . . . Did she have a big trap back then an all?

MELANIE. This fucking place.

RAILTON. It'll be alright, Mel.

MELANIE. Yeah it will cos I'm not having it.

RAILTON. Don't say that. Listen, I've got a whole house, haven't I? And I help me sister out all the time. I'm good at it. You won't have to worry about nothing.

MELANIE. No I won't cos I'm not having it.

RAILTON. You're scared, I know, but trust me. This is the best fucking luck. This is us chance to make everything alright, to have a future together. We can manage anything together, us.

MELANIE. There is no us.

RAILTON. Just think about it, please? Talk to me.

MELANIE. It's got nothing to do with you. Leave me alone.

RAILTON (*he pulls away from her*). That's not fair. It's not down to you. I've got rights.

MELANIE. No, I don't think so.

RAILTON. It's mine.

MELANIE. No, I don't think so.

RAILTON. What?

MELANIE. It's not yours. It's his.

RAILTON. Fuck . . . I don't believe you. You don't know. How can you know for sure?

MELANIE. I thought I was when I came back, when we –

RAILTON (*pacing*). Fuck . . . I don't understand . . . If you thought you were, why did you –

MELANIE. Cos I liked you, alright? Cos I wanted to forget him, move on –

RAILTON. No, I mean . . . Why did you go on the ride?

MELANIE. It doesn't matter. It didn't work anyway, did it? I've got to go away.

RAILTON. Fuck . . . No . . . Okay. Listen. (*Crushes fag out, crouches down, clasps her hands.*) Don't go away. Stay here. You're not thinking right. Think about it. We can keep it, just like it's mine. We can work summat out together. I could love it.

MELANIE. You could tell it wasn't yours easily enough.

RAILTON (*laughs, on the edge*). Ginger skips a generation.

MELANIE. It wouldn't be ginger, Railton. Or blonde.

RAILTON. Don't tell me. (*Clutching bottle, knuckles whitening.*) Don't tell me he was a –

MELANIE. He was British, but his parents were Indian. He met someone else out there. It wasn't all his fault, but he didn't fucking tell me until –

RAILTON. You should've fucking told me.

MELANIE. Why? Wouldn't you have spoken to me if I had?

RAILTON (*smashes bottle, still grips the neck*). I wouldn't have fucked you.

MELANIE. You can go now, Railton.

RAILTON. I bet she was one too, his other lass, wasn't she? Yeah, see. You've fucked multiculturalism and it's fucked you right back. Well, it serves you right. Flush the fucking thing away. I don't give a shit.

MELANIE. The truth at last. If it's white it can live, if it's not it can die. Well, it's better off dead anyway. I don't want to bring a kid into a world like that, a world filled with hate where you can't even have a fair without some racist thug planning a riot to ruin it. Yeah, Railton, I do remember Sheralyn Stack and yeah, she does have a big trap. She told me what you were up to and how she didn't think it was right cos her boss is a Paki and she's been having it off with him for the last six months but she wouldn't tell you cos she knows what'd happen. Cos she's scared that the next time you called by there'd just be a rattle of the letter box and the smell of burning. That's your community, Railton. That's your future. You couldn't love a kid. What would you do?

Fill it full of war stories about what Daddy did in the riots? Fill it full of hate and fear so nothing'll ever change? We don't need any more of your lot.

RAILTON. We don't need any more of his lot. They've took everything away from me.

MELANIE. Come on then, Railton. I've got the global community right here in my gut. Show me what you stand for. Come on, come on, show me your love. Show me your hate. Show me how you're going to make everything great again.

An electric moment as they square up. Her arms wide open. His tensed up, wired, wanting to. He explodes in a howl in her face and she closes her eyes, waiting for the blow . . .

The bottle smashes to the floor and RAILTON *follows it, crumpling up, crying.*

RAILTON. I want to go back. It was alright before.

MELANIE. No it wasn't, was it?

RAILTON. We was here last year, in the riots. A gang of Pakis versus a gang of us. Dad was in the car, parked up, cheering us on. I kept me thumbs on the outside of me fists like he taught me and I landed me a blinding right hook. This kid didn't know what hit him. He hit the floor. I looked down at him, gasping, pleading with his big black eyes. I could hear Dad yelling in me head, telling me to finish him off . . .

MELANIE. You didn't, did you?

RAILTON. I couldn't. I couldn't do it . . . How can you?

MELANIE (*pause*). It's not the same. It was a mistake.

RAILTON. I was a mistake.

MELANIE. I'm not ready yet. It's no kind of world –

RAILTON. There is no us and them, is there? There's just us and you. You you you, and you'd get rid of the whole lot of us if you could. Whites and Pakis, fucking up your nice life. No wonder you can't hear me. I can't reach you.

MELANIE. That's not fair.

RAILTON. I thought you was lost. I thought you was scared, but you're not. You're hard as nails you are. You're cold.

MELANIE. I'm trying to make things better.

RAILTON. I was gonna call off the riot. When I found out,
I was that happy, but now –

MELANIE. It's not my fault.

RAILTON. It's not fair. It's not fucking fair.

*When he looks up, she's gone. He runs up to the fair and
wrecks it. Ripping down the poster to an explosion of
smashing sounds and his anguished howl. When it's broken,
he staggers back, looks around and runs off. Blackout.*

SCENE FIFTEEN

RAILTON'*s house. He is slumped on the settee, surrounded by
cans, takeaway cartons, ashtrays and the scattered fairground
models. There is a knock at the door. He ignores it, curling up.
It gets louder, much louder.*

RAILTON. Break it down, you bastards. Come and get me.
I don't care.

*Silence. The knocking starts again, softer. He gets up and
answers the door to* MELANIE. *She carries a big rucksack.*

What do you want?

MELANIE. Have you been crying?

RAILTON. What do you want?

MELANIE. Can I come in?

She enters, and is shocked at the mess.

RAILTON. I was only expecting the pigs.

MELANIE. They don't know it was you who wrecked the fair,
yet.

RAILTON. Fucking useless, aren't they?

MELANIE. You tell me. They say the riot's been called off. Is
that right?

RAILTON. Can't have a riot without a fair, can we?

MELANIE. Is that why you called it off?

RAILTON. It weren't my doing. It'll amuse you to know the BNP's kicked us out as well. Sick of us using the party for us own ends. Local agenda endangering national strategy. Fuck 'em. They're the same as all the rest, just with shittier leaflets.

MELANIE. They're not the same, they're worse.

RAILTON. I don't care. Fuck 'em all.

MELANIE. It's probably for the best.

RAILTON. Everything's always for the best with you. When's this best gonna come my way?

MELANIE. Maybe today.

RAILTON. Why? Was you wrong? Is it –

MELANIE. No, it's not. And I'm still going away. That's why I've come to see you.

RAILTON. I don't do goodbyes no more.

MELANIE. My dad'll be round to see you later. I told him about you.

RAILTON. Great. (*Kicks one of the models.*) That's fucked it then. He'll kick me out for good now, won't he?

MELANIE. I told him you'd put the fair back together.

RAILTON. You what?

MELANIE. I told him you'd put it back together. Fix up what you can and fill in what you can't with your mates from the fair. The real fair.

RAILTON. Yeah right, what's the catch?

MELANIE. You're not stupid, you, are you?

RAILTON. Afraid not.

MELANIE. I said you'd be there to speak at the opening. I said who better to prove that we've moved on from last year. To prove that even you can move on.

RAILTON. You've completely fucking lost it, blondie.

MELANIE. That's what Dad said, more or less, but I said he should give you a chance.

RAILTON. I don't want your pity. Pride's all I've got left, ta.

MELANIE. I don't reckon either of us has got much to be proud of, do you?

RAILTON. I can't do it.

MELANIE. You have to, or the police will find out who did it and then you will be fucked.

RAILTON. Maybe I am stupid. Got you all wrong, didn't I?

MELANIE. I'm not hard, Railton. I'm just trying hard and I need your help.

RAILTON. I can't help you, Melanie. I can't move on. I'm stuck. Just leave me alone.

MELANIE (*picks up the broken model*). 'All movables of wonders from all parts.' Do you know that? . . . I looked it up. It's from that poem your dad taught you. Don't you know it all? . . . Fair's were mixed up even back then. It was the same. They just said it differently. Albinos. Painted Indians. The Negro with his timbrel.

RAILTON. His what?

MELANIE. Tambourine. Percussion workshop, innit?

RAILTON. Don't take the piss.

MELANIE. Maybe he'd be proud of you.

RAILTON. Maybe he'd turn in his grave.

MELANIE. You don't know. I don't know what's going on in my dad's head and he's alive. He spouts what he has to, to keep these people happy and shut those people up and I don't think he knows what he really believes in any more . . . He's looking old these days, don't you reckon?

RAILTON. Not as old as my dad looked.

MELANIE. But he was a lot older, wasn't he?

RAILTON. No, he wasn't. He was younger. He was only my age when they had me.

He sparks up a dog-end spliff from an ashtray. He passes it to her, and she takes a hit. She gives it back and stands up, wobbling slightly. She pulls on her rucksack.

MELANIE. My dad'll be round here tonight.

RAILTON. Where've you told him you're going?

MELANIE. I told him Rav was back in London –

RAILTON. Is he?

MELANIE. No, he's back in India.

RAILTON. Good. I do hate him, you know?

MELANIE. I know. So do I. But we'll get over it . . . Well, I
suppose –

RAILTON. Just go.

*She leaves. He pulls on the spliff too hard and starts
coughing, spinning out. He lies back, covering his face. The
lights dim, the old fairground music plays and* GEORGE
*enters, wearing his old ghost sheet and pyjama bottoms
once more. He creeps up to the settee.*

GEORGE. Click . . . click . . . click . . . Boo hoo hoo. (*Rocks
the Waltzer.*) What're you crying for, baby Railton? Just cos
of that posh bitch. Fuck her. She's nothing.

RAILTON. Fuck you. You're dead.

GEORGE (*sits down next to him and pokes through bones of a
takeaway carton*). That it then, is it? Show's over? Over my
dead body. Have you had your head turned by her fairytales?
Sucked in by her 'happily ever after' spiel at last?

RAILTON. What about your spiel?

GEORGE. You what?

RAILTON. The last showman will soon be as dead as the
dodo, you said, but they're not. Someone wrote that in
1870-summat and they still haven't died out, have they? Not
really. They've just changed. They've always changed, but
they're still alive. Bloody techno rubbish, you said, fucking
ragga, but I liked it.

GEORGE. What's it matter? Battle's over and Kid Hills's lost
for good, hasn't he? (*Gets up.*) No place in the nest for the
dodo, not with all these fucking cuckoos. You're a letdown
to me, son.

RAILTON. I'm tired of fighting, Dad, landing punches on nothing. Didn't it wear you out?

GEORGE (*sparks up, mouth still full of KFC*). Aw, sweet dreams, sorry for waking you. I only tried to tell you everything they hid from you.

RAILTON. But what've you hid?

GEORGE. What?

RAILTON. On the Revolution?

GEORGE. Don't recall no Revolution here, son.

RAILTON. On the ride last year, and in the riot, you were scared, weren't you? In the car, you were shitting yourself.

GEORGE. Was I fuck.

RAILTON. Yeah, that's what you said. That's how I wanted to remember you. But I remember you. Holding me hand that tight you almost broke me bones. You couldn't even scream, could you?

GEORGE. Not scared of nothing me.

RAILTON. You're scared of letting me down.

GEORGE. Why'd I be scared at a fair? (*Taps ash into carton.*)

RAILTON (*knocks the carton from his hand*). I don't know. You tell me, Dad. Maybe cos if the Pakis hadn't finished you off, the next ride might've. The next fag. The next fry-up. Is that the truth? Whose fault was it really? I need you to tell me. Were you trying to tell me owt or were you just screaming inside, 'I don't want to die, I don't want to die'? Were you just trying to keep your eyes open, keep your mouth open, keep breathing? Please. Tell me the truth, Dad. Cos I dunno what's real no more.

RAILTON *pulls the sheet off* GEORGE, *revealing him to be wearing a hospital gown and oxygen mask, weak and wheezing.* GEORGE *dies and reappears behind* RAILTON *using the Pepper's Ghost effect.* RAILTON *walks off, through the ghost.*

SCENE SIXTEEN

At the fairground, RAILTON *puts the fair poster back up,
gaffer-taped together and places* GEORGE*'s models around*
MELANIE*'s display. As he does this,* MELANIE *stands
barefoot in a hospital cubicle, getting changed back into her
clothes beneath a hospital gown. The different tunes, old and
new, play in broken snatches, spliced together, with gaps.
Separately,* RAILTON *and* MELANIE *exit. The music builds
to a climax, applause rings out and a spotlight comes up
centre stage.*

ANNOUNCEMENT. Ladies and gentlemen, to open this
landmark event, a fair for the future, please welcome to the
stage, Railton Hills.

*The applause dies. Silence. The stage stays empty for a long
time. Blackout.*

SCENE SEVENTEEN

The river by the fairground. RAILTON *is bent over, finishing
off heaving.* MELANIE *enters.*

MELANIE. Do you want me to hold your cap for you?

RAILTON. Don't look at me. Just leave us be.

MELANIE. They're all looking for you. I thought you might
be here.

RAILTON. I thought you'd gone.

MELANIE. I blew all my cash on a train ticket back last
minute so's I wouldn't miss your big speech. That's forty
quid you owe me, Batman.

RAILTON. That's the thing about Batman, he has no bloody
powers, has he? He's just a pussy in a mask.

MELANIE. What happened to the great showman?

RAILTON. I can do the show, Mel, but fuck the tale. What can
I say? I can't stand up there and tell them all what's wrong
and what's right cos I dunno no more. D'you know how I

got on with your action group? By slagging off the war. Oh yeah, we got on like a lock-up on fire about that one, but I'm not meant to drag the war up today, am I? Today's all about the future, but I don't even know what I can do tomorrow when this little action's over so what can I tell 'em? What can I say? Better let 'em get on with their fun. No one's listening.

MELANIE. I was listening. I was thinking . . . Listen, I think it's good.

RAILTON. You would.

MELANIE. I think you can start again now. Don't give up. Just pick a different party.

RAILTON. Yeah right, like who?

MELANIE. I don't know . . . The Greens?

RAILTON. Fuck off.

MELANIE. Sorry, anti-veg. I forgot. (*She gives him a bottle of water and watches him drink deep.*) Have you got it all out now?

RAILTON. Feel like it. Feel empty.

MELANIE. It's hard letting go, isn't it?

Pause. They are both holding their bellies.

RAILTON. You alright?

MELANIE. When I got back, my degree certificate had arrived. First Class Honours in knowing fuck all. I wanted to rip it up but my folks'd framed it, hung it up next to this photo of a grinning girl in a cape.

RAILTON. That'll be Batgirl.

Pause.

MELANIE. What're you going to do?

RAILTON. Dunno. Summat. Reckon I might go on a ride . . . What are you going to do?

MELANIE. Think I'm going to go home.

End.

FELT EFFECTS

Joy Wilkinson

Characters

NICOLA BELL, *various ages from three to eighteen*

ANGELA BELL, *various ages from six to eighteen.*
Also plays the GIRL

LIZ, *their mother, mid-forties*

PHIL, *Angela's father, mid-twenties.*
Also plays the MAN, *Nicola's father*

MO HUSSAIN, *mid-twenties.*
Also plays KRISHNA RAHMAN, *aged eight to eighteen,*
and the DOCTOR

Although the characters' ages change in different scenes, they should not imitate children, but should keep their normal voice i.e. remain at their upper age limit.

The play is set in a Lancashire town and in India.

This text went to press before rehearsals commenced so may differ slightly from the play as performed.

Three curtained-off sections, as in an A&E ward: two enclose beds, the third encloses LIZ's *lounge – a battered easy chair and TV.*

NICOLA *enters.*

NICOLA. Stop. (*Pause.*) Can you feel it? Can you feel anything . . . anything at all? (*Pause.*) Ten thousand earthquakes rip through the earth every day. And they don't all happen in far-off places where only Pakis and backpackers get hurt. Earthquakes happen here all the time. Three hundred a year. Most of them so tiny and deep down below the surface that no one seems to notice. Some of them are stronger, strong enough to rattle windows and doors and spill milk. In 1580, two people were killed by an earthquake in Dover. But 1580 was a long time ago and even Dover seems a long way from here. In 1931, a woman in Hull died of a heart attack suspected to have been caused by a big rift in the North Sea bed. But 1931 is still ancient and we hate people from Hull. Wrong side of the Pennines. Here, we register One on the Macroseismic Scale of Intensity. 'Not Felt.' Or at least, that's how it seems most of the time. Until one hits you.

MO *enters. He has a slight limp and wears a doctor's coat.*

MO. Nicola. Excellent. Come with me. There's something I want you to see.

NICOLA. Someone.

MO. What?

NICOLA. Whenever you say that, I think you wanted to show me a new piece of equipment. A new defibrillator or your new car or your little brown todger. But it's always a person. People aren't things.

MO. A todger is part of a person, Nicola.

NICOLA. Not so's you'd notice. And don't call me Nicola, Doctor Hussain.

MO. Nurse Bell. Come with me. There's a person I want you to see. I think you'll be interested. It's a very unusual case.

NICOLA. It?

MO. She. She. She. Come on. Follow me.

MO sweeps back the curtains around the central bed where the GIRL lies.

She was dropped off on the A&E pavement two hours ago: blacked out, battered and bruised. Poured out of a taxi, someone said. Usual thing, we thought. Drink. Drugs. But the blood's clean as a baby's. So we thought, accident perhaps. Domestic. Car wreck. But the injuries aren't consistent. Not with fists or a hit and run. And what else would someone want to hide? Why wouldn't her family or friends or boyfriend bring her in, if it was anything else? Strange. And then it got stranger. She won't wake up. We've checked everything and this is no coma. She's not unconscious. She's not dead. It's as if she's just . . . there, but not there. So we've got this girl with no name and no background with these mystery injuries who is in some fundamental sense not even really here. I think you can excuse me for the 'It' this time. When I saw her I thought of you . . . Not because you're an It, because of Christmas, because of what we were talking about before . . . ? Nicola? Nicola? Are you listening? What is it?

NICOLA. Level Two on the scale of intensity is 'Very weak'. Felt by very few people. Maybe even just me.

NICOLA opens the curtain to the second bed and climbs under the covers. The GIRL becomes ANGELA. She gets up and walks over to the bedside.

ANGELA. Morning, it. Does it still not talk? Is it the thickest little sister that ever forced its way through its mum's crossed legs? Mum says you didn't come out of her la-la like me. She squeezed you out of her arse like the turd that you are. You stink like a turd. Can you hear me, Nicola Bell? I hate it that you're allowed that name. That's my dad's name, not yours. Your dad's name was nothing. It was turd. So it's official, little it. You're shit. Can you hear me?

As NICOLA talks, ANGELA lights a cigarette and taps the ash on NICOLA.

NICOLA. I can hear, but I can't talk. I am three and Angela, my sister, is eleven. I've always heard sounds, but these were the first words I heard and understood. When it was all just sound, I think I was happy. I was hungry when Mum didn't feed me and I made some pretty bad sounds myself when I was ill and she wouldn't come, but other people's sounds were all the same and they sounded magical, like music, birdsong and laughter. Until I heard the words.

ANGELA. You are frogs and snails and snot and spiders and Aftab Mahmood's dandruff. You are the bits Aftab picks from his ears and flicks across the bus. You are the dogshit on my shoe that I can't scrape off and the stink of boys' farts that never goes away. You are an accident and Melanie Fenn says her mum says the shorthand for accident is 'X'. So that's your name. Miss X. Mistake. What is it?

NICOLA. I start to cry. I soon learn not to.

ANGELA. If you can't remember, I'll have to help you.

ANGELA *taps the ash from her fag, turns* NICOLA *over and is poised to brand the 'X' on her bottom.*

NICOLA. It got better when I got bigger. When I was bigger it was just nips and scratches and hair-pulling stand-offs. They didn't hurt. But those words did. However hard I try to block them out, I can still hear them.

MO. Say something. What is it, Nic?

NICOLA. Nothing.

MO. It looks like something. Or someone. Do you know this girl?

NICOLA. Doesn't she look like someone?

MO. A plate of meatballs maybe.

NICOLA. Someone. Someone you know.

MO. Give me a break, Nic. You know I don't watch TV.

NICOLA. I know you don't, but I thought that made you smart not stupid. Someone real, I mean.

MO. No. I give up. What are you trying to say?

NICOLA. Nothing. It's just strange, that's all. Like you said.

MO. It's bloody strange. I'd love to crack this one before they spirit her up to the ward and I never see her again.

NICOLA. Or before she dies.

MO. She won't die. The injuries are extensive, but not life threatening. If life's the right word. She's not critical, just strange.

NICOLA. Maybe she's dead already.

MO. She's not as strange as you, of course.

NICOLA. And don't call me Nic.

MO. I didn't mean bad strange. Strange can be good. I'm strange.

NICOLA. You're a fucking weirdo.

MO. What is it? Has she freaked you out? Or is it me? Is it because I mentioned Christmas?

NICOLA. It's nothing to do with that. It's nothing to do with you.

MO. I just thought you'd be interested.

NICOLA. I am. Don't I look it?

MO. You look freaked out and miserable.

NICOLA. I always look miserable. That's how students look.

MO. Not student nurses. You're supposed to smile for the old ladies. Revel in your caring role.

NICOLA. I don't come to the A&E to care. I do enough of that at home.

MO. Ah. How is your mother these days?

NICOLA. Save your revelling for the patients, Doctor. She's okay. She's okay as long as she'll never set eyes on this one.

LIZ (*voice from inside the second set of curtains*). My eyes are about to explode. For fuck's sake, hurry up.

NICOLA. Level Three. 'Weak.' Felt by a few people, indoors.

MO *pulls back the curtains.* LIZ *sits on the bed holding a cloth over her eyes.*

MO. Now then, Mrs . . . (*Reads notes.*) . . . Bell, there's no need to be rude.

LIZ. I'm dying in here. Wherever here is. I can't see shit. They just dumped me here and I can't see shit and it's been hours and I'm dying . . .

MO. You're not dying.

LIZ. How do you know?

MO. I'm a doctor.

LIZ. Doctors know fuck all. I even don't know why I came here. If I'm not dying, you'll finish me off one way or another . . . Here, are you a Paki?

MO. I'm a doctor.

LIZ. You are. Get your brown hands off me. Nurse?

MO. In your condition, I hardly think it matters what colour my hands are, Mrs . . . Ah. Are you any relation to Nicola Bell?

LIZ. Nurse!

NICOLA *joins them.*

NICOLA. Mum, what are you doing here?

LIZ. Leaving.

MO. You can't leave in your condition.

NICOLA. What is her condition?

MO. Let's take a look.

LIZ. Don't touch me.

MO. I don't want to touch you. It's my job.

NICOLA. You're wasting your time, Doctor. Let me have a look. Come on now, Mum. Can you open your eyes?

LIZ. No, I'm napping. Course I can, but I'm not doing. It hurts.

NICOLA. They're full of grit. Her eyeballs are like speckled eggs. What happened, Mum?

LIZ. He's still here. I can smell him. He stinks.

NICOLA. I know, Mum. Breathe through your mouth.

MO. You can't breathe through your mouth when you're kissing.

NICOLA. I wouldn't know.

MO. Neither would I thanks to this one.

NICOLA. Mo, please. Not now.

MO. Now seems like a good time, seeing as we're all here. Maybe fate's brought us together for a purpose.

LIZ. What's he on about?

NICOLA. Nothing, Mum. Ignore him. Tell us what happened.

LIZ. I haven't been drinking.

MO. I can smell you. You stink.

LIZ. I wasn't drunk. It was only lunchtime. I was watching the telly. Fuck all on, as usual. News. Why they think we want to watch the news at mealtimes I've no idea. Bits of brown bodies and blood showering all over the shop when I'm eating my meatballs. And there was fuck all news anyway. Nothing happens here since Princess Di passed on, bless her, so there was just the usual jabbering about the Arabs and the Pakis and that and I was just about to mute it when . . .

NICOLA. What?

LIZ. It sounds daft. Something . . . shook. I dropped the remote in my meatballs.

MO. You had a fit?

LIZ. No. It wasn't me shaking. It was the chair. Or I thought it was at first. Like in *The Exorcist*. When that lass is on the bed.

MO. Don't tell me you started to float.

LIZ. Course I didn't fucking float. I know it sounds daft, but it happened. And it wasn't just the chair. The telly was shaking too. The picture went mental.

MO. Like in *Poltergeist*?

LIZ. I mean it. The whole house was shaking. Only slightly. But enough to scare the living shit out of me. I stood up and dropped my meatballs all over the rug. I looked up at the ceiling to see what was happening and a load of shite fell down in my eyes. It felt like ground glass. The last thing I saw was my dressing gown covered in blood. I screamed like a psycho till I realised the blood was meatballs and the ground glass was plaster and then the shaking stopped. Took the ambulance an hour to come. That twat next door wouldn't give me a lift and I'd die sooner than call a Paki cab.

MO. She's drunk.

LIZ. Who do you think you are exactly? I'd hit you if it didn't mean touching you.

NICOLA. Even if she was drunk, it doesn't mean it didn't happen.

LIZ. I wasn't drunk then. I might have had one to steady me afterwards. I had to do something for the hour. Alone in blind agony, heart throwing upper cuts. It's such a comfort to have a caring daughter.

MO. It's a miracle more like. Almost as unbelievable as your account of your injuries.

NICOLA. Obviously something happened. She's in pain.

MO. For the first time in my career, I feel strangely disinclined to help.

LIZ. I don't want your help.

NICOLA. Yes you do. He can make you better. And you . . . do your job, Doctor, please. She's in pain.

MO. I know. I know she is, Nic.

NICOLA. Just don't give her an eye test on the girl next door.

NICOLA *goes through the curtains to the* GIRL. *She walks around the bed slowly, scrutinising her.*

Cinema 2000. Do you remember it? Big domes tiled inside with cinema screens. You had to strap yourself in and when the movie started, usually something about rollercoasters or space rockets, or earthquakes, the floor moved and the seats jerked about a bit. Cinema 2000. Seems so long ago now. It was the bollocks back in 1989 when I went on one at Peter

Pan World in Southport with my sister. We screamed our throats sore and at one point, we held hands. I stopped screaming then. Just for a second. Then she let go.

The GIRL *opens her eyes, as* ANGELA, *and screams.*

ANGELA. Mum. Nicola pulled my hair.

NICOLA. She pulled mine too. She's bigger than me.

LIZ. You're fatter. Leave your sister alone.

ANGELA. She's not my sister.

LIZ. She is a bit, love.

NICOLA. A whole half.

LIZ. I'm trying to watch the news.

NICOLA. You hate the news.

LIZ. But it's like you. It's there, so I have to make the best of it. Go and put the kettle on.

ANGELA. What's happening in the world, Mum?

LIZ. Horrible things, love. Wars and famines and earthquakes and all sorts of horrors.

ANGELA. I like horror films.

LIZ. Yeah, but they've got a good story, haven't they? This is just for the sake of it. It makes my feet hurt. Iron bars drilling through my feet. Thank God we live in England. Thank your dad he was a good man and gave us a safe home.

NICOLA. What did my dad give us?

LIZ. A load of trouble. Have you got that brew?

ANGELA. I'd like to live somewhere else, sometime. Somewhere hot.

LIZ. Like Southport? We had fun in Southport, didn't we?

NICOLA (*gives the brew to* LIZ, *digs bottle out of the chair and adds a tot*). It was well ace. Do you remember Peter Pan World, Ang?

ANGELA (*points at the TV*). Somewhere like there.

LIZ *jerks.* NICOLA *spills the drink.*

NICOLA. I'm sorry, I'm sorry, I'll sort it out.

She runs out.

LIZ. Tell me you're lying to me, angel. Do you know how far off that is? You'd have to fly for a start. Tell me you're lying.

ANGELA. I'm lying.

NICOLA *returns with a cloth and a box of frozen fishcakes which she presses to* LIZ's *wrist.*

NICOLA. For the burn. It'll make it better.

LIZ. Angie baby, don't do that to me. My poor heart can't take it. I hardly like letting you leave the house. I feel like keeping you inside for ever, my pet. Locking you up like a beautiful bird . . . What the frig are you doing, girl? That's tomorrow's tea when you've finished.

NICOLA. Nothing. Sorry. Can I go out to play now?

LIZ. Go on, clear off.

NICOLA. Earthquakes measuring Magnitude Four were felt in Warwick in the year 2000, in Arran, Strathclyde in 1999, and in Norwich in 1994. Another stopped production on oil platforms in the North Sea in 1985 and another caused minor damage in Kintail. Unless, like me, you have a real need to seek out facts about these events, you will have no idea that they happened. You probably won't even know where the fuck Kintail is. So it has always amused me, in a twisted sort of a way, that Level Four is classified as 'Generally Observed'.

MO. I get the feeling your mother doesn't like me.

NICOLA. Top marks for observation. But don't worry. It's nothing personal. She hates all Pakis. And doctors.

MO. I get the feeling she doesn't like you much either.

NICOLA. Yeah. That's one hundred per cent personal.

MO. Would it help if I told her I'm not a Paki at all? My family's from Bangladesh.

NICOLA. It'd make things much worse. If they could get any worse.

MO. Would it help if I told her I was born in Accrington?

NICOLA. It didn't help me.

MO. You don't hate Pakis do you, Nic?

NICOLA. I hate everyone.

MO. I used to say that. Well, I never said it, because I hated everyone so I had no one to say it to. But I could show you some pretty nasty diatribes online. Venting my spleen onto the screen, getting back at my parents, teachers, classmates, those sadistic bastards at med school. What I wrote'd put your mum to shame. It puts me to shame now. Now that I know there's good people too. People I like.

NICOLA. You mean those geeks you play internet chess with? They're not people. They're pixels. You can't like pixels.

MO. I didn't mean them.

NICOLA. Leave it out, Mo. Not today.

MO. Why not today? What is it, Nic? It's not just your mum. It's that girl, isn't it? Who is that girl? You know her, don't you? I can feel it.

NICOLA. Getting a lot of feelings today, aren't you, Doctor?

MO. It's a strange day. I can't tell if it's good or bad strange yet.

NICOLA. It's bad. Too bad.

MO. Don't call me Doctor, Nic.

LIZ. Doctor! Quick! He's waking up.

MO, *as the* DOCTOR, *pulls back the curtains around the second bed.* LIZ *is sitting by the bedside, clutching the hand of* PHIL, *who lies in the bed.*

He's going to make it . . . isn't he?

DOCTOR. I'm sorry. It's impossible, Mrs Bell. I explained. I'm afraid it's too late for your husband.

LIZ. But he's waking up.

DOCTOR. He wants to talk to you. I'll leave you two alone.

The DOCTOR *leaves.* PHIL *stirs.*

PHIL. Lizzie.

LIZ. I'm here, baby. Angie's here too. She's playing next door.
I told her, Daddy would see her soon. She's too little to
know what's happening, but she knows something's
happening. She was awake before I got to her. Bolt upright
from a nightmare, screaming and shaking. You'll be able to
see her soon won't you, baby?

PHIL. I want to tell you what happened.

LIZ. I know what happened. The policeman said. That Paki
taxi driver smashed into you. Ran you both off the road.
Killed himself before I could get my hands on him. But he
didn't kill you, did he, baby?

PHIL. He couldn't, that's what I want to tell you. He couldn't
kill me.

LIZ. I know it. I knew that doctor was a lying get. One of his
lot died and he wants us to suffer too. Does it hurt, baby?

PHIL. No. I . . . I feel good.

LIZ. Angie? Angie, Daddy's going to get better, come and
look.

LIZ *collects* ANGELA *from the bed next door. When they
return,* PHIL *has died.* ANGELA *goes to touch him. He
jerks suddenly. She pulls back and looks up at* LIZ. PHIL
lies still.

NICOLA. Level Five. 'Strong.' Objects fall over. Things break.

ANGELA *leads* LIZ *to the lounge.*

ANGELA. The remote's broke.

LIZ. I know. I broke it. I smashed it to bits.

ANGELA. That was silly. Now you'll have to get up to put the
telly on and you hate getting up.

LIZ. Do you miss your dad, Angie? Do you remember him?

ANGELA. Sort of.

LIZ. Do you remember waking up when you knew he'd been
hurt?

ANGELA. No.

LIZ. No. I've seen this programme on it. You don't think you remember, but it's still in there, deep down. You've got this gift, this link with him. That's why you're special, baby. You're special anyway, aren't you?

ANGELA. I dream about him sometimes.

LIZ. See, that shows you. You're so lucky. What does he look like? What does he say?

ANGELA. I don't see him. I just feel him. I feel he's happy.

LIZ. Is he? Do you think he is? I hope so, but I don't know. I can't dream no more. I just have nightmares. Sometimes I wake up and I think he's just gone to the loo in the middle of the night, like he always had to after the pub, and I lie there waiting for him to come back. I wait and I wait, listening to the cistern, waiting for the flush and for his footsteps to come shushing back across the landing, careful not to wake me. But he never comes. And the bed's so cold without him. It's too big.

ANGELA. You still fall out of it.

LIZ. You think once you've got someone who doesn't fuck around, someone you can trust, who calls when he says he'll call, who actually wants to marry you and have babies and is actually proud to tell people he's going to marry you and have babies. You think that's that. You've got it cracked. And then you get married and have a baby and he's still there, still calling, still proud, you can't bloody believe it. You think, this doesn't happen. I must be dreaming. And then you realise you are. Something else happens, out of your control. Someone else does something that's nothing to do with you, some Paki taxi driver doesn't pass his test, and suddenly, you wake up. And it's all gone.

ANGELA. I'm still here.

LIZ. Yes, my angel. You're here, thank God. And you have his eyes.

ANGELA. Can I go out to play, Mum?

LIZ. No, Angie. Stay here, stay safe inside with me.

NICOLA. There were several earthquakes in Britain that reached Magnitude Five. It was a 5.8 that killed those two poor Dover souls in 1580 and way back in 1185, a 5.5 destroyed part of Lincoln Cathedral. Back then, they probably thought it was the wrath of God, hurled down on their church in punishment for their sins. They built it up again quick-sharp, bigger and better. Fives are pretty damn scary, but I've still never met anyone who remembers feeling one, even though there was one in 1990 that sent tremors across the whole of England and Wales, which even includes here. I asked my mum if she felt the biggest onshore British quake of the twentieth century, which happened on July 19, 1984. The day I was born. She said she didn't feel a thing. It was the same story nine months earlier, the night she met my dad. Completely numb, she reckons. She let him have a good feel though.

A doorbell. PHIL *as the* MAN *approaches the lounge. Angie opens the curtain to him.*

MAN. Hello love, is your mummy in?

ANGELA. She's always in. So am I.

MAN. That can't be very good for a young lass.

ANGELA. I'm a beautiful bird.

MAN (*dirty laugh*). Too right you are.

ANGELA. Mum, there's a strange man at the door.

MAN. I'm here about the TV.

LIZ. Don't keep him on the doorstep, Ang, bring him in.

MAN. It's cold out there.

LIZ. Would you like a drink?

MAN. Love one, cheers.

LIZ *pulls a bottle of brandy from the side of her chair.*

LIZ. Fetch another glass from the kitchen, Angie.

MAN. I thought you meant a brew.

LIZ. She can't make brews. I won't have her messing with the kettle.

MAN. You've twisted me arm. Go on then. Cheers.

ANGELA *brings a glass in.* LIZ *fills it. They chink glasses.*

LIZ. I like that sound. 'Chink.'

MAN. Don't like Chinks, though, eh?

LIZ. What? Oh. (*She laughs.*) You're funny, you. I haven't laughed since . . . ages ago.

MAN (*chinks her glass again and swigs*). Just the two of you, is it?

LIZ. I thought I'd have to wait till she got older to hear that sound again. I think when she's older, I'll be able to go out again, and we'll go out together, like sisters.

MAN. I'd tell you that you looked like sisters, except she's just that bit too young. You look good though.

LIZ. Give over.

MAN. Straight up. Give me another drink and then the bullshit'll really start to flow.

ANGELA. Are you going to fix our telly?

MAN. Indeed I am. What seems to be the problem, miss?

ANGELA. The remote's broke and when you switch it on with the real switch it goes mental, like on *Poltergeist.*

MAN. Maybe you've got a poltergeist.

ANGELA. Really?

MAN. No. It's just the wiring.

LIZ. Can you fix it so there's some decent stuff on and not just news and wogs playing sport all the time?

MAN. See enough wogs round here without having to watch them on the telly, aye?

LIZ. That's one of the comforts of staying in.

MAN. They're good at sport, blinding at cricket, I'll give them that, but do you know what? They're shit at fixing tellies. There's one at our place, Paki Fred his name is, and he knows fuck all. Can hardly speak English, never mind wire a plug. I swear they only took him on for what's it, quotas. Everyone's scared stiff of being called racist these days. Not me. They can call me what they want and I'll call them what they are. That's what they came here for, wasn't it? Free country. If they don't like it, they can fuck off home.

LIZ. They're not really all round here, are they?

MAN. Oh aye. Was one on the street just now as I pulled up. Tried to run the bastard over, but he was a slippery little shit. They are, aren't they? You want to watch who your little girl plays with. And keep your doors and windows locked.

LIZ. This house is safe, don't you worry. It's the only place that is.

MAN. No place like home, aye?

LIZ. It's not like home with the telly broke though. Go on, fix it up so it's good as new and Paki-free.

MAN (*laughs*). I can get it working alright, but I'm not sure about the Pakis, love. I tell people I work in TV, but in reality it's not a very powerful role. Just aerial and set maintenance from here to Blackpool.

LIZ. Feels like life and death when you don't get out.

MAN. I could take you out.

ANGELA. Don't you have to stay in and look after your little girl?

MAN. No, love. I'm not married. But if I had one, I'd want her to be just like you.

ANGELA. A beautiful bird.

MAN. Exactly. (*Raises his glass.*) To a couple of beautiful birds.

Laughs, chinks his glass with LIZ's *and drains his drink.*

LIZ. You remind me of someone. Close your eyes.

MAN (*eyes closed*). You smell good.

LIZ. I smell of drink. Do you want some more?

MAN. I wouldn't mind. It's warming me up a treat.

LIZ. Me too. Open your eyes.

She stands and takes off her dressing gown. She is only wearing a short nightie.

Go out and play, Angie.

ANGELA. I don't want to. It's cold. I want to watch telly.

MAN. There's fuck all on.

LIZ. Go on, clear off.

LIZ *and the* MAN *climb onto the second bed.* NICOLA *closes the curtain.*

MO, *as* KRISHNA, *approaches* ANGELA.

KRISHNA. What's your name?

ANGELA. Fuck off, Paki.

KRISHNA. No, that's my name. What's yours? What are you doing here?

ANGELA. I live here. What are you doing here?

KRISHNA. I live here. Brewer Street. I play here all the time, but I've not seen you before.

ANGELA. You killed my dad so I have to stop in with my mum.

KRISHNA. I'm sorry. I didn't mean to. When did I do it?

ANGELA. Two years ago. When I was six.

KRISHNA. I lived in India two years ago. That's where I'm from.

ANGELA. Where's India? Is it hot?

KRISHNA. So hot you'd singe.

ANGELA. I'd like to singe. I'm freezing.

KRISHNA. Here.

He holds out his parka. Hesitantly, she takes it.

Do you want to play something?

ANGELA. I don't like sports.

KRISHNA. Neither do I.

ANGELA. Oh. I thought you were good at them.

KRISHNA. As if. I'm well crap. I broke my tooth on a cricket ball. Do you want to see?

ANGELA. Yeah. Go on.

He opens his mouth wide. ANGELA *peers in.*

That's ace. Does it hurt? (*He gargles 'no'.*) Can I feel it? (*He gargles 'yes'.*) Ooh. That feels ace.

KRISHNA. I hate cricket.

ANGELA. Can you fix tellies?

KRISHNA. I don't know. I've never tried. I've made a burglar alarm for my room though, out of a clock and a pudding bowl.

ANGELA. That sounds well ace. My mum could do with one of them for our house. She's para about Pakis breaking in.

KRISHNA. Why?

ANGELA. She says it's not safe around here.

KRISHNA. It's not. I almost got run over by some twat in a van just now and I don't think it was by accident. He wasn't a Paki though. He was white.

ANGELA. Oh. Sorry.

KRISHNA. S'alright. I'll let you off cos I like you.

ANGELA. Do you?

KRISHNA. What's your name?

ANGELA. Angela Bell.

KRISHNA. My name is Krishna Rahman.

ANGELA. That's an ace name.

KRISHNA. It's an Indian name. If you come to my house, I'll show you India. I've got a globe that lights up. It's well ace.

ANGELA. It sounds it, but I'm not meant to talk to Pakis.

KRISHNA. Pakis aren't from India. Pakis are from Pakistan and their proper name is Pakistanis.

ANGELA. How do you know?

KRISHNA. It's on my globe. Come and see it. I can show you my burglar alarm an all.

ANGELA. My mum'll go mental.

KRISHNA. She won't see. Your curtains are closed.

ANGELA *looks back at her house.*

ANGELA. Oh.

KRISHNA. How come you don't have to stop in with her tonight?

ANGELA puts on the parka.

ANGELA. Cos she's giving you a chance. Where's your house?

ANGELA and KRISHNA go off.

NICOLA goes to the curtains around LIZ and the MAN and listens. She kneels on the floor and listens to it. She puts her hands on the floor.

NICOLA. Can you feel anything?

There is an abrupt series of squeaks from the bed inside. They quickly cease and the MAN slips out and away, fastening his belt.

Not really.

NICOLA opens the curtains. LIZ is asleep. ANGELA enters and goes to touch her. LIZ jerks suddenly in a nightmare. ANGELA pulls back. They both scream.

LIZ. Angie? What is it?

ANGELA. I thought you were . . . like dad.

LIZ. Oh no love, come here.

They hug.

You smell funny.

ANGELA. You smell funny. You smell of that man.

LIZ. Don't smell it, angel. Breathe through your mouth. Is he downstairs now?

ANGELA. No. He's gone. And he didn't even fix the telly.

LIZ. Gone?

ANGELA. He said he couldn't fix it. He said we'd have to get in touch with the manufacturers.

LIZ. He said a lot of things. A pack of lies.

ANGELA. Is it always bad to lie, Mum?

LIZ. Course it is. Why? You haven't been lying to me, have you, Angie?

ANGELA. No. *I* haven't been lying to *you.*

LIZ. What do you mean?

ANGELA. The proper name for Pakis is Pakistanis.

LIZ. What? What you on about, Angie?

ANGELA. Nothing. Forget it.

ANGELA *climbs down off the bed and leaves.*

LIZ. I was having a nightmare. My feet hurt, Ang. I need a drink. Ang? Get me a drink. I need a drink.

MO *enters and draws the curtain around* LIZ.

MO. Nicola, can you please come and explain the hospital's policy on alcohol to your mother?

NICOLA. She knows it off by heart. She heard it enough times at the antenatal clinic. It's a wonder I was born with any brain cells.

MO. Some might say you weren't.

NICOLA. Fuck off, Doctor.

MO. I'm joking, Nic. I know you only pretend to be an ignorant pig. I know how swotty you are. I've seen inside your locker.

NICOLA. What have you seen?

MO. Books. Loads of them. Not just medical books either. Geography, most of them looked like.

NICOLA. Geology.

MO. Same thing.

NICOLA. If you think brain surgery's the same as colonic irrigation.

MO. You aren't going to abandon nursing I hope. The NHS would be lost without you.

NICOLA. I'm not going anywhere, so you can tell the NHS he needn't worry.

MO. He is worried. Because he knows there's something wrong. He knows about swotting and how it's not always just about passing exams. How it's sometimes about hiding from things.

NICOLA. You're not a psychologist, Doctor. And it's not about hiding from things. It's about finding things out. Do you understand? It's like, I'm trying to find out . . . I'm trying to make sense . . .

MO. Of what?

NICOLA. All my work, all my swotting, everything revolves around . . .

NICOLA *glances at the* GIRL*'s bed.*

MO. Her?

NICOLA. You wouldn't understand. I don't understand.

MO. Try me. I might. My mother didn't drink.

NICOLA. It's nothing. Forget it.

LIZ. I need a drink!

NICOLA. You'd better go and help her.

MO. Come with me.

NICOLA. No, she likes you more. Go on.

MO *goes to tend to* LIZ. ANGELA, *as the* GIRL, *sits up in the central bed. She reaches out and pushes the vase on the bedside table slowly, slowly, to the edge, until it falls off and smashes.* NICOLA *runs to pick up the pieces.*

GIRL. Accidents.

NICOLA. No.

GIRL. You are frogs and snails and snot and spiders . . .

NICOLA. And you're dead.

GIRL. Not in your head.

NICOLA. Who are you?

GIRL. Miss X.

NICOLA. I'm Nicola Bell. I'm not listening.

GIRL. That's why you work here. That's why you swot. That's what your everything revolves around.

NICOLA. You're dead.

GIRL. But why accidents, Miss X? Because you hate them? Because you want to understand them? Because you want to stop them?

NICOLA. Stop.

GIRL. Because you are one.

ANGELA sweeps everything off the bedside table.

LIZ. I need a fucking drink.

NICOLA tears open the curtain around the bed where LIZ lies, legs crossed, in agonising labour. MO as the DOCTOR tries to tend to her. NICOLA watches.

I don't want it, I don't want it. I want a drink.

DOCTOR. That's what got you here in the first place, Mrs Bell.

LIZ. No it wasn't. It was an accident. It was you. It was you that got me here. You and your lot. Can't you kill it? Isn't that what you're good at? Can't you kill the fucking thing?

LIZ and the GIRL thrash in pain and scream simultaneously. NICOLA drops the pieces. The DOCTOR administers a sedative to LIZ. She and the GIRL stop and fall still. MO draws the curtains around LIZ.

As NICOLA speaks, she clears up the pieces, replaces the vase and draws the GIRL's curtains.

NICOLA. Level Six. 'Slightly Damaging.' Have you felt it yet? (*Pause.*) I don't just have geology books. I have everything I can lay my hands on. History, religion, science, fiction, science fiction, even film. In the fifties and sixties, film directors shot their wad trying to find ways to make viewers react to what was going on onscreen. William Castle rigged up electric devices to the seats in some cinemas where his monster flick *The Tingler* was running. The monster in this case was Fear, in the form of a parasite which lodged itself in the spinal column and could only be removed by screaming. When the monster conveniently found its way into a cinema, Castle flicked the switch and got the audience screaming with a full-on electric shock. 'Do you have the guts to sit in this chair?' boomed the posters. What did this poster say? Did we warn you beforehand? Did we rig anything up? These days, the devices are so small, you can't even feel them, you're nice and comfy . . . until we flick the switch. Then you'll feel it. Or can you feel it already, out there in the dark? Fear. Just a little. Danger. Coming closer. What might happen to you tonight? Nothing, as usual. Or something. Someone.

MO. Nicola. Quick. Come with me.

Pulls the curtains back around the GIRL.

NICOLA. She's worse.

MO. I know.

NICOLA. You said she wouldn't die.

MO. She won't. I hope. She had a fit.

NICOLA. What kind of a fit?

MO. I don't know. We're running tests. She started screaming. I ran in and the bed was shaking.

NICOLA. Like in *The Exorcist*?

MO. No, that's not right. She was shaking.

NICOLA. Not the bed?

MO. No. Shit. You were right about today. This is bad strange. I think I'm finally losing it.

NICOLA. Did she wake up? Did she say anything?

MO. She won't wake up. What's the matter? You've gone white.

NICOLA. I am white.

MO. No more bullshit, Nic. It's not funny any more.

NICOLA. I'm not laughing.

MO. No. You're hurting and I want to help.

NICOLA. Because it's your job?

MO. You know why. You know you can trust me. If you know something about this girl, tell me now.

NICOLA. Level Seven. 'Damaging.' Tall things, fragile things, start to fall.

MO, *as* KRISHNA, *gets in bed with the* GIRL *who becomes* ANGELA.

KRISHNA. Hey angel, did we make the earth move or what?

ANGELA. I wanted to keep my eyes open but I had to close them, right at the last minute. And then it was all darkness. Shifting darkness. And I felt . . .

KRISHNA. What?

ANGELA. I don't know . . . as if the world was lighting up inside.

KRISHNA. You sure it wasn't just my globe lamp shining through your eyelids?

ANGELA. Don't take the piss, Kris. I can't describe it. It just felt . . . good.

KRISHNA. Good?

ANGELA. I felt the same as you, part of you.

KRISHNA. In that case you'll definitely have to come to India with me.

ANGELA. My mum will go mental.

KRISHNA. You're not eight any more, Angie. You're eighteen next month. And your mum has the little freak to take care of her.

ANGELA. She doesn't like Nicola. She likes me.

KRISHNA. I like you. I love you. Come with me. It was your idea. You want to see the temples.

ANGELA. I want to see everything.

KRISHNA. I want to see the temples with you. I'm not arsed about the temples without you. I've seen enough temples to last me a lifetime. And if you're right, lots of reincarnated lifetimes.

ANGELA. I want to see the sea and the mountains. The rivers and the forests. It's strange. I feel like I've seen them before somewhere. In my head, in my belly.

KRISHNA. On the telly, more like. Go on, come with me. Please?

ANGELA. I suppose I could just not tell her. Tell her something else.

KRISHNA. Tell her you're off to an NF Training Camp. She'll give you the money herself.

ANGELA. I don't like lying.

KRISHNA. Where did you tell her you were going tonight?

ANGELA. To the Megabowl with Becky.

KRISHNA. So what's the difference?

ANGELA. I'm safe here.

KRISHNA. She wouldn't think so. The burglar alarm wouldn't be much comfort when she clocked me. Come on, Ang. You're lying to yourself. You're already on a different planet as far as she's concerned. You don't belong in her twisted little world. You belong with me.

ANGELA. Yeah. I know. I know you'll look after me.

KRISHNA. We'll look after each other. It'll be ace.

ANGELA. I can still feel it, Kris. Can you?

KRISHNA. I don't think so. It's different for men.

ANGELA. No. Hold me. Close your eyes. Can't you feel it?

KRISHNA. I can definitely feel something starting to stir.

They laugh.

LIZ (*from inside her curtain*). Angie?

NICOLA *closes* ANGELA'*s curtain and exchanges glances with* MO.

Angie? Is that you?

NICOLA. No. It's Nicola. Is your hearing fucked as well as your eyes?

LIZ. It's all fucked. You remember that story I read you when you were little, about the little bird and the sky falling in?

NICOLA. No. That wasn't me.

LIZ. What's it come to when you're not safe in your own home?

MO. Seventy per cent of accidents happen in the home.

NICOLA. I thought it was more.

LIZ. Don't talk to him. Come in here. Talk to me. Why are you talking to him?

MO. Don't go. Talk to me.

LIZ. I don't know how you stand it. Those bastards killed your father.

NICOLA. Not my father.

LIZ. Those bastards killed your sister.

NICOLA. Level Eight. 'Very Damaging.' Walls crack.

　　NICOLA opens ANGELA's curtain. ANGELA is packing.

ANGELA. Fuck off, Nic. I'm busy.

　　NICOLA doesn't go. She walks around the bed, picking over the items ANGELA is packing: sarong, bikini, suntan lotion, sandals.

NICOLA. Isn't it winter?

ANGELA. It is here, but it's not there.

NICOLA. I got a gold star in Geography.

ANGELA. So?

NICOLA. If it's winter here, it's winter in Spain.

ANGELA. Haven't you heard of winter sun?

NICOLA. In the southern hemisphere.

ANGELA. Fuck off, swotty little turd. You're such a fucking freak. I don't know how come you got so swotty. Your dad certainly didn't have any brain cells to spare.

NICOLA. You don't know my dad.

ANGELA. I could have shagged him myself if I wanted to. He's still going strong. Dipping his wick wherever he can then fucking off in his crappy van. A string of kids by remote control from here to Blackpool.

NICOLA. You're going with that Paki.

ANGELA. I'm afraid I don't know any Pakistanis.

NICOLA. The one from Brewer Street. Krish somethingorother.

ANGELA. He's an Indian, so you know where you can shove your gold star for Geology.

NICOLA. Geography.

ANGELA. Right up your swotty arse.

NICOLA. You woke me up. The other night. I was having a nightmare. It felt like the whole house was shaking. And when I woke up, it wasn't the whole house, it was just your bed. It was you shaking, in your sleep. And you said his name, over and over. 'Ooh Kris, Kris, Kris.'

ANGELA. Fuck off, Nic.

NICOLA. You're going to India with him.

ANGELA. Top marks, but I'm all out of gold stars so fuck off. You're just jealous. You know no one'll ever want you. Not even a crippled fucking weirdo. No one wanted you in the first place.

NICOLA. Mum'll go mad.

ANGELA. Fuck right off, remote control kid. Turd on my shoe I can't scrape off.

NICOLA. Don't change the subject.

ANGELA. I'm not. That is the subject, isn't it, Miss Clever Turd? You're a fuck-up so you want to come in here and fuck things up for me.

She pushes NICOLA.

NICOLA. I'm not a fuck-up.

She pushes ANGELA back.

ANGELA. You are. You're a freak. An accident. A fucking disaster.

NICOLA. At least I'm not a Paki-lover.

They go for each other's hair and cry out.

NICOLA. Mum. Angela's pulling my hair.

ANGELA. Say anything and you're dead, I swear.

NICOLA. I'll tell and then you're dead. You and your Paki.
You're dead and then Mum'll see who's best.

ANGELA. Mum. Nicola's pulling my hair.

LIZ (*from inside curtain*). Leave your sister alone.

They part. ANGELA *gets into bed, becoming the* GIRL
again.

NICOLA. She wasn't my sister.

MO. I didn't know you had a sister.

NICOLA. I don't.

MO. Your mum just said . . .

NICOLA. Half-sister.

MO. And this is her?

NICOLA. She's dead. She was killed in an earthquake in India
eight years ago.

MO. Then this can't be her, can it?

NICOLA. I know it can't. I know it, but . . . I don't know
everything, do I? And when you first showed her to me, I
felt . . . something. Look at her, Mo. Who does she look
like?

Pause. Now MO *takes his time to scrutinise her.*

She looks like me.

MO. Maybe.

NICOLA. Yeah, yeah, I'm fatter, I know. But she does. And
her injuries. Not consistent with a fist or a hit and run, you
said. How about a fall? How about a crush? How about an
earthquake?

MO. Nicola, it can't be. You said she was dead. Long dead. In
India for God's sake.

NICOLA. I know, but . . .

MO. Throw your film books away, Nurse. This is real life. People don't come back from the dead. I don't treat ghosts.

NICOLA. Don't call me Nurse, Mo, I mean it.

MO. I'm sorry, but I thought you were smart.

NICOLA. I'm trying to be, I'm trying but it doesn't add up. Who saw the taxi pour her out?

MO. Someone.

NICOLA. Who? Why does nobody know her? Because her only family is here. Mum and me. What was it you said? Maybe fate's brought us all together today for a purpose.

MO. I didn't mean it. I don't believe in fate.

NICOLA. You don't know though. Maybe, you said. Maybe you were right. Maybe she's come here to fuck us up. To get me back.

MO. What for?

NICOLA. Because I killed her.

MO. But you said an earthquake . . .

NICOLA. It was me. It was my fault. I did it.

Loud blast of TV interference. LIZ *sits in her chair waving the remote.*

LIZ. You've broken it. Nicola! Sort it out.

NICOLA *bangs the TV. The interference stops and the news starts.*

Sometimes I think it was worth all the bother just for your TV repair skills.

NICOLA. Really?

LIZ. No. Was there any post?

NICOLA. No. Sorry.

LIZ. I should sue that postman. And his bum chums in Spain.

NICOLA. I got another gold star today, Mum. In Biology. Do you think I could be a nurse?

LIZ. Do you think she's alright? I do worry.

NICOLA. I could be your nurse, and look after you for ever.

LIZ. She's not gone for ever. She'll be back in a month and then she can look after me. Did you go to the shop?

NICOLA. Yes.

LIZ. Did they serve you?

> NICOLA *gets a brandy bottle from a carrier bag.*

> I should call the police. Serving booze to a ten-year-old. No respect for our laws. None of them. Give us that here.

NICOLA. I don't like them, Mum. Their shop smells funny.

LIZ. I know, love. Breathe through your mouth.

NICOLA. Angie went in that shop.

LIZ. Do you think she misses me?

NICOLA. Mum, Angie went in that shop all the time. She liked it.

LIZ. Look what Princess Di's got on. Beautiful.

NICOLA. She loved it.

LIZ. Angie might have a tan too. Weather report said it was snowing in Spain but you know what bollocks they talk. Angie said it would be scorching. Please God she won't burn.

NICOLA. Do you worry about me, Mum? When I go out?

LIZ. I should never have said yes. She should have stayed here. God knows what can happen out there.

NICOLA. Do you ever worry about me?

LIZ. You see it all the time on *Watchdog*. Holidays from Hell. Food poisoning, perverts, sharks, earthquakes . . . Do they have them in Spain?

NICOLA. She's not in Spain. She's in India. She lied to you. She's in India with a Paki and she's letting him fuck her.

> LIZ *drops the remote. It smashes on the floor.*

LIZ. Now look what you've done.

NICOLA. Level Nine. 'Destructive.' Some houses, the weaker ones, the ones with crappy foundations, collapse. You can't always see the cracks. You think you're safe. Major earthquakes sometimes happen on blind faults – there's no sign on the surface and then suddenly . . . Have you felt a Level Nine here? They happen. All the time. Continuously. Don't you notice your house slowly collapsing around you? You think, I'll fix that and this and that, but you're busy and you don't fix it. Or them. And then it's too late.

MO *sways on with two glasses and tinsel round his neck.*
NICOLA *takes one.*

MO. Nurse Bell, could you please explain the hospital's policy on alcohol to me?

NICOLA (*pissed, giggling*). Don't do it, Doctor Hussain. Especially if you're not used to it, especially not bright pink Christmas punch of unknown origin.

MO. You don't drink normally?

NICOLA. It's against my religion.

MO. Really?

NICOLA. The religion of 'don't turn out like your fucking mother'.

MO. Shit. My mother doesn't drink. I should make more of an effort.

He chinks her glass and necks his drink.

NICOLA. Won't you get in trouble with your Paki church?

MO. I don't go to church. Or the mosque. And I know you know it's called a mosque. I've seen you reading the Koran in paperback, for some reason I can't fathom.

NICOLA. Have you been spying on me, Doctor?

MO. I spotted you on your first day and took up spying on your second.

NICOLA. You fucking weirdo.

MO. Crippled fucking weirdo, get it right, Nurse.

NICOLA. I never said that.

MO. I don't care. I'm used to it.

NICOLA. You do care. You're just pissed.

MO. So are you thinking of converting to the Paki church?

NICOLA. No. I'm just interested.

MO. You're interesting.

NICOLA. No. I'm not.

MO. Neither am I. This is the first time I've been out all year, except to go to work.

NICOLA. This is work.

MO. That's how boring I am. Do you know what I do when I'm not working, Nurse Bell?

NICOLA. Do I want to know?

MO. I stop in and I play online chess with people I've never met.

NICOLA. You're more interesting than me then. I just stop in. I stop in and I read, on my own, except for my mum, but she doesn't count.

MO. You're interesting to me, Nurse Bell. Tell me why you read what you do. Do you believe in God? Any god?

NICOLA. I'm celebrating Christmas.

MO. *I'm* celebrating Christmas. (*Chinks glasses again.*) Do you believe in God?

NICOLA. I don't know. That's what I'm trying to find out. I'm trying to figure it all out.

MO. Shall I tell you a secret, Nurse Bell?

NICOLA. Call me Nic.

MO. There is no God. There is no Allah. There is no afterlife or reincarnation or limbo or ghosts. This is all there is.

NICOLA. How do you know that? You can't know that for sure.

MO. Do you know why I limp, Nic? The first time I ever came to this A&E department, I was dead. I got hit by a car when I was a kid. I shouldn't have been running across the road, but it was the driver's fault. Some rally-boy twat who hadn't passed his test. He knocked me out and left me there and by the time the ambulance picked me up, I was dead. My heart had stopped. I was dead for seven minutes until they jump-started me again, in a bed on this very ward. And do you know what happened to me in those seven minutes, Nic?

NICOLA. No.

MO. Nothing. No voices, no lights, no glowing tunnels. No hovering by the air vent, embarrassed by my little battered body. No god of any name, sex or colour. Just dead. Seven minutes completely gone from my life. And when I woke up, I wanted to be a doctor. Because it was doctors who had power over life and death. It was a doctor who brought me back from the dead and made me better again, almost. So this is my religion. This and this and this.

He touches his chest, his head, and then, tentatively, her face.

NICOLA. So if you're not religious, how come you don't normally drink?

MO. Because I'm a doctor and it's bad for you.

NICOLA. So are you feeling bad now, Doctor Hussain?

MO. Call me Mo.

NICOLA. Shall I tell you a secret, Mo?

MO. Yes.

NICOLA. I'm really pissed.

MO. Is that it? That's not a secret.

NICOLA. No, I mean, I'm really pissed, because I wouldn't say this otherwise. I shouldn't.

MO. Say it.

NICOLA. I've never kissed a Paki.

MO. I've never kissed a white girl.

NICOLA. I've never kissed anyone.

MO. Neither have I.

LIZ. Nicola?

NICOLA. My mum'd go mental.

MO. So would mine, but let's not turn out like our mothers, eh?

LIZ. Nicola.

NICOLA. I can't.

MO. I like you.

NICOLA. Stop it. You're pissed.

MO. Good. I was wrong. It's not all bad for you. It feels good, doesn't it?

NICOLA. No. No, it's bad. I shouldn't drink.

MO. It's Christmas.

NICOLA. This is a mistake. I should go.

MO. No.

NICOLA. I'm going home.

MO. It's not bad.

NICOLA. It is. I am.

LIZ. Nicola. Help!

A loud smash as LIZ *stands up and her plate of meatballs hits the floor.*

NICOLA. I'm coming, Mum. What is it?

LIZ. The telly. On the telly . . .

NICOLA. Level Ten. 'Very Destructive.' Many houses collapse.

LIZ. My beautiful bird.

NICOLA. The worst earthquake in the history of Southern India hit on September 30, 1993. Almost ten thousand people were killed and many thousands more were injured. The disaster was especially shocking because it was in the part of India with the lowest risk of earthquakes. People thought they were safe. Most were killed because their homes weren't built to withstand any tremors. When the quake began, even though it only lasted a matter of minutes, seconds, everything collapsed.

LIZ. Go back to it, go back to it. Fucking news. Two minutes. He's talking about the Queen now. The fucking Queen. Go back.

LIZ gets up, lurches to the TV and hits it as she shouts. Her bottle falls and smashes. The TV cuts to interference.

MO *as the* DOCTOR *opens the curtains around* ANGELA *who is in bed with her eyes closed. He feels for her pulse. Listens to her heart. She opens her eyes.*

DOCTOR. How do you feel?

ANGELA. I . . . I feel good.

DOCTOR. What's your name?

ANGELA (*pause, smiles*). Mrs Krishna Rahman.

DOCTOR. The man with you was your husband?

ANGELA. The wedding stopped before the end. The walls started to crack. But yes. He was.

DOCTOR. I'm sorry he didn't make it. Him and too many others.

ANGELA. He's alright. They're all alright.

DOCTOR. This place will never be alright again. The hospital spills out for miles. Hundreds of miles. The rivers have flooded. The sea is bloody. The mountains move with dying bodies. People. Children.

ANGELA. It will be alright.

DOCTOR. What are you doing over here, so far from home?

ANGELA. This is my home.

DOCTOR. Where are you from? Where is your family?

ANGELA. I held him and I closed my eyes. I breathed in his smell. I love it. And then the earth moved. (*She laughs, coughs.*) Do you believe in God, Doctor?

DOCTOR. Not a god that kills. I'm a doctor. I believe in saving lives. I believe in this.

He touches the dressed wound on her head.

ANGELA. Yes. You're right, but that's not all, is it? That's only part, only the start. I believe in everything.

DOCTOR. Where are your family? We need to get in touch with them, to tell them you're going to make it.

ANGELA. I'm not going to make it, Doctor. It's impossible. You know that. This is my home. Bury me here.

DOCTOR. I need to tell your parents, your mother and father.

ANGELA. My dad already knows. My mum will soon. If she switches the telly off for one single fucking second.

She laughs, coughs, coughs up blood. LIZ *screams and smashes the telly.*

NICOLA. Level Eleven. 'Devastation.'

LIZ. Angie.

LIZ *stands by the centre bed where the* GIRL *lies.* MO *and* NICOLA *join her.*

NICOLA. You can see.

MO. Apparently she's still having trouble.

LIZ. It's Angie. Oh my baby. How? Did the bastards bring you back at last?

MO. You can't bring people back from the dead, Mrs Bell.

LIZ. Don't say my name. Don't speak to me. Look at her face. What have you done to her?

NICOLA. Stay calm, Mum. Your heart . . .

LIZ. My heart's beating, for the first time in years, I can feel it. She's come back. I prayed for this.

NICOLA. You don't believe in God.

LIZ. I do. I do now.

MO. You're wrong.

NICOLA. Maybe she's not.

MO. We don't have time for maybes, Nicola. She's dying.

LIZ. No!

MO. Mrs Bell, listen, you need to help me.

LIZ. Get off me, murderer. Both of you. Can't you leave us alone?

MO. This isn't Angela. But she is someone and she's dying and we don't have much time. If you know anything that can help us reach her family then tell me now. Please, Liz?

LIZ. Fuck off, Paki.

MO. Have you had another daughter?

LIZ. There's only Angie.

MO. Another daughter besides Angie and Nicola. A daughter you gave away? An accident perhaps?

LIZ. No.

NICOLA. I was the only accident and she kept me. I suppose it never crossed her mind to give me away.

LIZ. I wish it had. I crossed my legs.

NICOLA. You should have crossed them nine months earlier.

LIZ. I should have wrapped them around Phil so tight he could never leave home.

MO. It's not Angie.

LIZ. I need a drink.

NICOLA. You should be glad you kept me. I'm the one who got your drinks. I'm the one who stayed.

MO. What about your father? Nicola, couldn't this be your father's daughter? Didn't he leave . . .

NICOLA. A string of unwanted kids from here to Blackpool. Yes, I guess I've got hundreds of brothers and sisters somewhere, but I don't know them . . .

MO. And they don't know you. And if you had an accident, who would bring you to the hospital?

LIZ. Look at his eyes.

MO. His?

LIZ. Her eyes. His beautiful eyes.

NICOLA. She's right. They're not my eyes. My crappy grey eyes from my grey ghost dad. They're her dad's. They're Angie's.

LIZ. It's Angie.

MO. It can't be.

LIZ. How do you know? How can you know? You don't know anything about us. You don't know how it feels to lose someone you love. To have them taken away, twice, by animals like you. To know you'll never ever see them again, no matter how much it cuts you in two. To be left with nothing, wanting nothing but to be numb. I need a drink.

MO. It was drink that started all this.

LIZ. No. It was you. Why don't you fuck off home and fuck each other and kill each other and leave us alone? Leave us alone.

MO. I can't and I won't, because it's my job and because I'm part of it too.

NICOLA. No, Mo.

MO. Yes, Nic. I'm part of it. I love your daughter, Mrs Bell.

LIZ. No.

MO. It's the truth and I want you to know it. Stop all this bullshit and face up to the truth. All of it. I'm not an animal. Nicola isn't a mistake. And this isn't Angie. You know who this is. Figure it out, Liz. Stop praying and think. Isn't there another possibility? One that doesn't involve God or ghosts. One that bears some relation to the real world.

PHIL enters. He is on the phone, with a drink in his other hand.

PHIL. Angie? It's Daddy. Is your mummy there? . . . Lizzie? I'm just calling because I said I would. Sorry to be so predictable. What are you up to, Lizzie? . . . Is there anything on? . . . Fucking news. Put a video on . . . Don't scare yourself. How's my baby girl doing?

The GIRL gets out of bed and runs up to him. He ruffles her hair as he talks.

Give her a goodnight kiss from me, I might be back late. Got a lot of work to finish up here. Then I'll hurry on back to you . . . Don't worry. I'll be careful. I'm always careful. I love you, Lizzie.

He switches the phone off and takes a long swig. He kisses the GIRL's head.

And I love you too, but it's time for you to clear off to bed. Where's your mum?

GIRL. Pissed watching telly.

PHIL. I've got some catching up to do. I can't stay long.

PHIL *exits.*

NICOLA. Level Twelve. 'Catastrophic.' Everything destroyed. (*Pause.*) Remember those ten thousand people in India, who included my backpacker sister and her Paki lover? You probably don't remember actually, but anyway, forget them. They were nothing. In Japan, in 1923, an earthquake killed one hundred and forty-three thousand. And in China in 1556, eight hundred and thirty thousand died. People. But 1556 is a long time ago and China is a very long way away from here and they were all Chinks anyway. And all these numbers . . . I've swotted for so long that I can't count them any more, they're just shapes and the people blur and the map's just pictures and the words don't mean anything and I understand less and less the harder I try to focus. Maybe Mum did fuck up my brain cells before I was born. Maybe I am just a total fuck-up, an accident, a disaster.

GIRL. You are frogs and snails and snot and spiders and Aftab Mahmood's dandruff. You are the dogshit on my shoe and the stink of boys' farts. You are sugar and spice and all things nice and you are my tan and my eyes and the sweet smell of Krishna wrapped around me in hot rain. You are the heat and the cold and the river and the sea. You are me and I am everything and everyone and I'm alright. I am good and bad. I feel. I felt the earth move and the priest stopped and I looked up at the ceiling to see what was happening and something happened to my eyes, someone, and there was no fear, just love. And all the smells and the colours and the sounds were the same and they sounded magical, like music and laughter and the birdsong of beautiful birds. And I saw that everything is an accident. Everyone. And I closed my eyes and I breathed him in and I was him.

NICOLA. What did you say?

MO. I said what if she's not your daughter? Or your sister?

LIZ. No.

NICOLA. No. She said something. I heard her. No, I felt her.

MO. What if your husband wasn't a saint? Look, Mrs Bell.
    Look at his eyes. Her eyes.

LIZ. Don't speak my name.

NICOLA. Stop. Can you feel it?

LIZ. Don't touch me.

MO. He lied and he cheated on you and he had another child.

LIZ. No. I don't believe you.

MO. And what if he wasn't killed? What if he was the killer?
    Maybe he killed that man.

LIZ. Stop.

NICOLA. Stop.

MO. Not a Paki. Or a taxi driver. Not a thing. A man.

NICOLA. What if nobody killed anybody and it was all just an
    accident? Not a mistake. A gift. A chance . . .

MO. Liz . . .

LIZ. Fuck off, Paki . . .

    LIZ *picks up the vase to hurl at* MO. NICOLA *holds the*
    GIRL*'s hand. The* GIRL *sits bolt upright.*

GIRL. Stop.

    The GIRL*'s bed shakes. The* GIRL *thrashes. Her heart
    monitor flat-lines.*

    At the same time, LIZ *clutches her heart and collapses.* MO
    catches her. NICOLA *catches the vase before it smashes.*

    DOCTORS *rush on and pull the curtains around the* GIRL,
    MO *and* LIZ.

NICOLA. Did you feel it? I felt something. Did you? The
    switch flicked. Did it work? Close your eyes . . . Anything?
    Or has it faded already? Or were you too far away? It's hard
    to feel anything from far away . . . There's something in
    Seismology called a Love Wave. Named after someone
    lucky enough to be called Love. I can remember the

definition: 'A major type of surface wave with a horizontal motion transverse to the direction of propagation.' Fuck knows what that means, but I like the sound of it. It sounds like . . . it sounds. I think, no, I don't think. I just know I'd know a Love Wave if I felt it. If I can just stop . . . and feel it.

MO *leads* LIZ *through the curtains to her chair. He sits her down tenderly and administers a sedative.*

MO. How are you feeling?

LIZ. Better, I think. I feel . . . I feel good. (*She looks up to the ceiling.*) Did the sky fall down?

MO. Yes, but we can fix it again. Like we fixed you.

LIZ. You couldn't fix her though, could you?

MO. No. I'm sorry, Mrs Bell. She didn't make it. Whoever she was. I'm sorry, but you know it couldn't have been Angie and you aren't left with nothing. The good news is your daughter is alive and well. And I'd be grateful if you made the most of her. For my sake. I don't know what it's like to lose someone I love and I don't want to find out just yet. Do you understand, Liz?

She doesn't respond. He sighs and tries to put the remote in her hand, but she rejects it. Instead, she takes his hand.

NICOLA *opens the curtains to the* GIRL*'s room and looks at the empty bed. She walks around it slowly.* MO *enters.*

NICOLA. Are you spying on me, Doctor?

MO. Course I am. I'm a right fucking weirdo, me.

NICOLA. Good.

MO. Actually I'm keeping an eye on you for your mother.

NICOLA. Is that the truth?

MO. Maybe.

Pause. NICOLA *touches the pillow.*

NICOLA. Are you pissed off that you didn't manage to crack the mystery in time?

MO. No. I'm pissed off that she died. But they'll run all the tests downstairs. They'll solve it. Her.

NICOLA. And if they don't?

MO. You'll have to keep swotting and solve the mystery yourself.

NICOLA. I don't think so. I don't think I've got that long to spend swotting and I've got a feeling I won't know the answer until it's too late to tell anyone.

MO. And then will you tell me?

NICOLA. Maybe I won't need to.

MO. Nic?

NICOLA. She looked like me.

MO. No. She didn't. Your eyes are more beautiful . . . Nic?

NICOLA. Mo?

MO. Can you feel it? Anything at all . . . ?

Pause.

She drops the vase.

They look at each other.

NICOLA. Close your eyes.

As they move closer, the lights fade to black.

End.

A Nick Hern Book

Fair and *Felt Effects* first published in Great Britain
as a paperback original in 2005 by Nick Hern Books,
14 Larden Road, London W3 7ST in association with Floodtide

Fair and *Felt Effects* copyright © 2005 Joy Wilkinson

Joy Wikinson has asserted her right to be identified as
the author of this work

Cover image: Jodie Coston / Acclaim Images

Typeset by Country Setting, Kingsdown, Kent CT14 8ES
Printed in Great Britain by CLE Print Ltd, St Ives, Cambs PE27 3LE

A CIP catalogue record for this book is available from
the British Library

ISBN-13   978 1 85459 903 2
ISBN-10   1 85459 903 8